MW01010172

WHAT

# Every 2nd Grade Teacher Needs to Know

Margaret Berry Wilson

**About Setting Up** AND **Running a Classroom**

CENTER FOR RESPONSIVE SCHOOLS, INC.

All net proceeds from the sale of this book support the work of Center for Responsive Schools, Inc., a not-for-profit educational organization and the developer of the *Responsive Classroom*® approach to teaching.

The stories in this book are all based on real events in the classroom. However, to respect students' privacy, their names and many identifying characteristics have been changed.

ISBN: 978-1-892989-38-3
Library of Congress Control Number: 2010927985

Cover and book design by Helen Merena
Photographs by Paula Denton and Jeff Woodward, and © Alice Proujansky and Peter Wrenn.

Thanks to the teachers and students of Mary C. Dondero Elementary School, Portsmouth, New Hampshire; Mount Pleasant Elementary School, Nashua, New Hampshire; Kensington Avenue Elementary School, Springfield, Massachusetts; Six to Six Magnet School, Bridgeport, Connecticut; University School of Nashville, Nashville, Tennessee; and Wissahickon Charter School, Philadelphia, Pennsylvania, who welcomed Northeast Foundation for Children to take photos in their classrooms.

Center for Responsive Schools, Inc.
85 Avenue A, P.O. Box 718
Turners Falls, MA 01376-0718

800-360-6332
www.responsiveclassroom.org

Third printing 2019

Printed on recycled paper

# CONTENTS

# Knowing
# Second Graders

I am always struck by the way second graders strive to make sense of the bigger world and to make their personal worlds as orderly and safe as possible. Among other things, they put a great deal of faith in facts. When I meet them before school starts, they are often nervous and get through our opening conversation by listing facts to define themselves. (*"I have two regular brothers and two stepbrothers. They are my stepbrothers because my parents are divorced, and my dad's new wife has children."*) They also have an amazing capacity to remember details and often seem slightly discomfited when their teachers forget facts they consider essential to stories being read aloud. (*"Don't you remember, Ms. Wilson? In chapter one, Malcolm put an origami star up his nose and had to go the nurse?"*) And they like to read series books (it's safer to stick with what they know!)—in order. I will never forget the horror of many of my students when upon discovering that our class library lacked the next book in a particular series, I suggested that they just go ahead to the next one. Not possible for many second graders!

These and many other unique characteristics of second graders make it a fun and satisfying year to teach. Second graders' devotion to facts and order helps them retain much of what they learn, put algorithms and other learning structures to use, and work hard to follow instructions. They value their end products and often do careful, thoughtful work.

However, second graders' love of order, facts, and safety also can lead them to be perfectionists and to be quite risk averse. They need help from their teachers so that they can learn to balance their desire for order and perfection with an appreciation for surprises and mistakes. Second graders benefit from seeing their teachers make mistakes and laugh them off. They need us to understand and empathize with their craving for order while gently pushing them to also see the joy in random events, surprises, and changes.

I wrote this book to help you bring such understanding and gentle nudging into your classroom so that you and your second graders can get the most out of this valuable year. You'll find information on a variety of topics, including arranging furniture, planning and teaching lunch and recess routines, building community, and engaging parents in classroom life. All my recommendations consider common strengths and challenges of second graders. Whether you're new to teaching or an experienced teacher switching into second grade, the ideas and tips in this book will help support you and your students.

## Children Are Different at Different Grades

Research tells us, and we educators know from our own observations, that all children develop and change in certain ways as they grow up. Over time, their physical and verbal abilities change. They also experience other changes, such as their preference for working and playing alone or with a group, how open or averse they are to taking risks, or what they think is funny. We must know such common characteristics to teach our students well. With this knowledge, we can design work that is appropriately challenging and engaging for them; anticipate what they will need in the way of furniture, supplies, and room setup; and know how to respond when things go wrong.

I was dramatically reminded of the importance of paying attention to where children are developmentally when I became a second grade teacher after teaching first grade for four years. The first graders I taught had happily drawn self-portraits whenever assigned. I thought the same assignment would be a safe, engaging activity for the beginning of second grade as well, one that would tell me a great deal about these students' talents, personalities, and interests. I was dismayed when, instead, the task brought on anxiety, many

*Research tells us, and we educators know from our own observations, that all children develop and change in certain ways as they grow up.*

2

requests for mirrors so that the children could study themselves, and virtual incapacitation. What made this task, so enjoyable the year before, so arduous now?

Suspecting that the answer had something to do with the differences between most first and second graders, I did some reading on the subject. My readings confirmed what I had been observing. First graders typically love trying new things, work at a fast pace, and are not too concerned with the quality of their end products. For them, producing a self-portrait was no big deal. On the other hand, I learned that just a year later most children need to be accurate, dislike taking risks, and hate making mistakes. To draw themselves, these second graders would require more support than I had provided. No wonder the self-portrait assignment was such a struggle for so many of them!

This experience taught me to scaffold so that second graders could be more successful with open-ended assignments like drawing self-portraits. I also learned to incorporate knowledge of second grade characteristics into my teaching in many other ways. The next section describes many of these characteristics so that you might begin to do the same.

## Common Characteristics of Second Graders

Of course, to teach second graders well, you will need to know about the many unique qualities typically seen in second graders in addition to their love of order and structure, avoidance of risk, and perfectionist tendencies. The table on pages 5 and 6 details these other common characteristics. As you use this table, keep these points in mind:

■ **Human development is complex.** Even scientists who study it do not yet fully agree on the means by which humans grow socially, emotionally, linguistically, or cognitively. Most theorists describe the process as involving a dynamic interaction between a person's biological disposition and many other environmental factors—from the historical era in which a person grows up, to the person's culture, family, and the institutions he or she encounters (like schools, places of worship, and the media). The table is not intended to ignore this complexity but instead to offer you a bridge between theory and the reality of classroom teaching.

■ **Every child is unique.** As a result of the complex and dynamic process of development, no two children—not even identical twins with the same genetic make-up—will develop in the same way or at the same rate. Also, a child may develop must faster in one area than in another. For example, a particular second grader might have social-emotional behaviors very common among second graders (such as preferring to work alone or with one friend rather than with a large group) but cognitive behaviors more like those of a third grader (such as increased interest in logic).

4

■ **The table gives you a practical frame of reference.** It lets you prepare for teaching second graders and have a resource if something puzzling comes up. For instance, once you start teaching second grade, you may notice that many students' writing is very tiny. Rather than expending a great deal of energy trying to figure out why they're writing that way or how to "fix it," checking the table and seeing how typical this behavior is will allow you to focus your energy on other aspects of your students' writing besides its size.

■ **The table is not about what's "normal."** It's not intended to limit your thinking about students' potential, to help you make decisions about whether a student is "normal," or to lead you to ignore the needs of students who differ from other second graders. For instance, although many second graders need fairly quick and manageable assignments, you may encounter students who appear ready to take on bigger, more ambitious projects. By all means, go with what you see and give students what they need.

To learn more about child development, see the resources in the "About Child Development" section on page 112.

# Second Graders

| Common Characteristics | School Implications |
|---|---|

## *Social-Emotional*

| | |
|---|---|
| ■ Are self-focused, with distinct likes and dislikes. | ■ Show appreciation and understanding of students. Private conversations and notes mean a great deal. |
| ■ Can be serious, moody, or shy. | ■ Use playfulness and humor to lighten their tension. |
| ■ Dislike taking risks and making mistakes. | ■ Stick to predictable schedules and routines. Provide coaching if these must change (assembly, special event, guest teacher, etc.) |
| ■ Need security and structure. | |
| ■ Like working and playing alone or with one friend; often find group work overwhelming. | ■ Give mostly individual or one-partner assignments. |
| ■ May change friendships quickly. | ■ Provide private, quiet spaces (reading corners, desks with privacy dividers). |
| | ■ Assign seats, but rotate them frequently to encourage working with a variety of classmates. |

## *Physical*

| | |
|---|---|
| ■ Are more coordinated physically (better at sports, for example); get confidence boost from newfound success in physical activities. | ■ Provide plenty of opportunities for outdoor games. |
| ■ Can focus on small, close-up things; have difficulty seeing things far away, such as the board. | ■ Minimize tasks involving copying from the board. |
| ■ Often write and draw compact, small letters and figures; find it difficult to write big. | ■ Accept small handwriting (expecting big writing may be counterproductive). May be best to wait until they're older to teach cursive. |
| ■ Have many aches, pains, and injuries (real and imagined). | ■ Show understanding and reassurance about aches and pains. |

5

CONTINUED

| Common Characteristics | School Implications |
|---|---|

### Cognitive

| | |
|---|---|
| ■ Try hard to make their work perfect. | ■ Expect high-quality finished products. |
| ■ Enjoy repeating tasks and reviewing learning. | ■ Give open-ended assignments (write about a topic in their own words, investigate a phenomenon in science, etc.), but spell out clear steps to follow. |
| ■ Enjoy inquiry and hands-on tasks; often wilt under time pressure. | ■ Eliminate or greatly limit timed assignments. |
| ■ Need frequent check-ins with the teacher. | ■ Give a heads-up that a work period is about to end. |
| ■ Like to classify and sort. | ■ Let students see classmates' works in progress (to realize the importance of process as well as end product). |
| ■ Enjoy board and computer games. | ■ Teach students ways to check in with you while you're working with others. |
| | ■ Provide a range of board games, puzzles, manipulatives, blocks, and craft materials. |

### Language

| | |
|---|---|
| ■ Show significant growth in listening skills. | ■ Make use of students' growing listening skills—gradually lengthen instruction and discussion periods (5–10 minutes at start of the year, 15–20 minutes by end of the year). |
| ■ Speak with precision. | |
| ■ Enjoy one-on-one conversations, especially with adults. | ■ Provide listening centers and audiobooks. |
| ■ Show great interest in words and have rapidly developing vocabularies. | ■ Weave word play, word games, and vocabulary activities into many parts of the day. |

6

The information in this chart is based on *Yardsticks: Child and Adolescent Development Ages 4–14*, 4th ed., by Chip Wood (Center for Responsive Schools, 2017), and is consistent with the following sources:

*Child Development Guide* by the Center for Development of Human Services, SUNY, Buffalo State College, 2002. WWW.BSC-CDHS.ORG/ FOSTERPARENTTRAINING/PDFS/ CHILDDEVELGUIDE.PDF

"The Child in the Elementary School" by Frederick C. Howe in *Child Study Journal*, Vol 23, Issue 4, 1993.

*Your Child: Emotional, Behavioral, and Cognitive Development from Birth through Preadolescence* by AACAP (American Academy of Child and Adolescent Psychiatry) and David Pruitt, MD, Harper Paperbacks, 2000.

# What About Developmentally Younger and Older Second Graders?

In any one classroom, you'll find a range of chronological and developmental ages—children with earlier and later birthdays or children who do not show the common second grade characteristics regardless of where their birthdays fall. If you have developmentally or chronologically younger students, they may be more like first graders. Here's just a sampling of those younger characteristics, along with how you might adjust your teaching for these children.

- **Highly social, energetic, and competitive.** Provide lots of noncompetitive, cooperative activities. Require them to be quiet only when it's absolutely necessary, and then only for a short while.

- **Physically very active yet quick to tire.** Give lots of movement breaks, and keep assignments short. Give students space to spread out their work if possible.

- **Often in a hurry and excited to learn, but not too concerned about creating a perfect product.** Reinforce their efforts and understand that they'll grow into caring more about their finished products.

- **Talkative and enjoy explaining their thoughts.** Provide many opportunities for them to explain how something happened and how things work.

Some students in your class might show common third grade characteristics. Here are some examples and implications for your teaching.

- **Enjoy socializing and working in groups.** Structure large-group projects, but expect a mix of socializing and work.

■ **Have improving hand-eye coordination.** Allow time for practicing handwriting, drawing, and crafts.

■ **Are increasingly interested in logic, classification, and how things work.** Provide hands-on math and science lessons that involve the use of concrete tools to explore abstract concepts.

■ **Have rapidly expanding vocabularies and love to explain their ideas.** Provide many opportunities to write stories and poems and record in writing what they've learned in social studies and science.

## How to Use This Book

You can use this book in various ways. For example:

■ **Read cover to cover.** If you have plenty of time and know you will be teaching second grade in the coming year, there are advantages to reading the book from beginning to end. Doing so will give you the big picture of how the common characteristics of second graders can inform the decisions you make before school starts and as the year progresses. You may want to take notes or mark key passages so that you can return to them if you forget some strategies you wanted to try or just need another look at a behavior or situation.

■ **Right now all I want to know is . . .** Of course, sometimes you don't know what grade you're teaching until right before the school year starts. In that case, you might just want to go for the information you need right away. Maybe you want some good ideas for how to connect with your students and their families right at the beginning of the year. In that case, go to Chapter 5, "Communicating with Parents." Or you might want to work on setting up the classroom in a way that accommodates second graders' needs. Read what you need, and then return to the other chapters later when you have more time.

Regardless of how you use this book, my goal is to help you, not overwhelm you. Start with ideas or practices that seem easy or make the most sense to you. You don't have to try everything at once. As you get comfortable with some basic strategies, bring in a few more. Remember that mistakes are how we learn, and children will survive if we do mess up (for instance, by giving them a self-portrait assignment that brings them to tears!). Often, mistakes are what make us better teachers.

## Last Word

Sometimes, we teachers focus on all the things that stand in our way or that we cannot do. But teaching second grade offers us so much that we *can* do. It's an exhilarating grade to teach. Among other things, you will be able to help your second graders make sense of the world, have the structure and order they crave, and most important, have fun while learning. Get to know your students—developmentally and individually—and enjoy them. Finally, be kind to yourself and forgive your mistakes. Not only will doing so help you, but it will also provide a powerful model for your students.

## CHAPTER 1

# Classroom Setup

Second graders need a well-designed, stable classroom where they don't have to worry about where they'll sit, where things are, or whether they'll be able to find what they need. Basically, they need to feel "at home" in the room. I knew I'd achieved this "at home" feeling one gloomy winter, when we had indoor recess in our classroom for days at a time. When the sun came out, I was so ready to get outdoors. But many of my students had more mixed reactions—they loved having the extra time in their classroom and even wanted to have lunch there!

To give your second graders this feeling of comfort and security, keep in mind their need for structure and stability as you design your classroom. This chapter will guide you in thinking carefully about how to arrange the furniture, what materials second graders need, where to put supplies, and how to set up classroom displays so that second graders can thrive starting right from the first day of school.

Once you choose an overall classroom design, stick to it as much as possible—second grade is typically not the year when children like to try out new furniture arrangements or new locations for classroom supplies every month. That said, you'll learn from this chapter that you can, and should, use small changes in room setup (such as periodically changing seat assignments) to stretch these children in healthy ways socially and academically within the confines of a safe room design.

# Arranging the Furniture

## *Whole-Group Circle*

Ideally, the whole-group circle space anchors a second grade classroom. A large, comfortable circle on the floor is a perfect place for teaching second graders. Being together with classmates and their teacher in a circle where everyone can see everyone else gives second graders the sense of comfort, security, and belonging they need. Each morning, the children can gather in a circle for a meeting to launch the day and set a positive tone for the day's learning. I find that the *Responsive Classroom®* Morning Meeting provides a valuable structure and purposefulness to these morning gatherings. Whether or not you hold a formal morning meeting, having a circle area will give you a place to launch the day with your students and do other community-building activities.

**Learn More About Morning Meeting**

*The Morning Meeting Book*, 3rd ed., by Roxann Kriete and Carol Davis (Center for Responsive Schools, 2014).

*80 Morning Meeting Ideas for Grades K–2* by Susan Lattanzi Roser (Center for Responsive Schools, 2012).

The circle comes into play throughout the day as well. In my second grade circles, we have learned how to use math manipulatives and played whole-group math games, examined our tiny caterpillars with hand lenses, and felt sad together at the end of the book *The Tales of Despereaux*.

A circle also fits second graders' physical development. These children's inability to see well at far distances requires that we keep them close to us for whole-group instruction and sharing of ideas. Compared with the more traditional approach of having second graders sit at their desks for all instruction, having them sit in a circle on the floor will enable them to better see charts, interactive writing, or a teacher's writing.

If your room is small, it may be tempting to forget about having a circle. I urge you instead to see if you can save space by the way you set up the students' desks. (See "I Don't Have Room for a Circle!" on pages 14 and 15 for more ideas.)

The circle can be used for a variety of instructional purposes. As a general rule, you should introduce or open most lessons in the circle, have students work independently at their desks or other areas of the room, and then come back together as a circle to close the lesson.

## Ways to Use the Circle

| Curriculum Area | Use the Circle for . . . |
| --- | --- |
| Social | Class meetings, practicing social skills and routines, group games and activities |
| Writing | Mini-lessons, sharing work, interactive writing |
| Reading | Read-alouds; partner chats about books, poetry, and other shared reading experiences; dramatizing books; mini-lessons about reading strategies |
| Math | Exploring manipulatives, mini-lessons, teaching games |
| Social studies | Mini-lessons on using texts and resources, examining artifacts, acting out historical and political events |
| Science | Mini-lessons on using texts and resources, examining materials, introducing experiments or hands-on activities |

# "I Don't Have Room for a Circle!"

Unfortunately, this is not an unusual dilemma for teachers. Here are some possible solutions:

## Create a temporary meeting area.

At meeting time, the children move desks and other furniture to open up a large space for a circle. After the meeting, the students return the furniture to its original place. With adequate teaching and practice, children will be able to do this setup and takedown in just a few minutes.

Three keys to making a temporary meeting area work:

- **Choose carefully.** Choose a spot with as little furniture as possible. Any furniture should be easy for students to move.

- **Use props to define the area.** An easel pad typically works well. Ideally, the easel pad would stay put and serve as the point from which the meeting circle grows.

- **Teach furniture moving.** Use Interactive Modeling to teach and practice how to move the furniture carefully, cooperatively, and quickly. Try turning the practice into a game, such as beating the clock.

### Interactive Modeling

See Chapter 2, "Schedules and Routines," for a full explanation of Interactive Modeling.

## Create it once, use it twice.

Have children move furniture to make room for a circle at the end of the day and gather the class for a "closing circle," in which the children reflect on their day, share about their work, or plan together for the following day. After the meeting, leave the space open—don't move any furniture back. The next morning, the space will be ready for a meeting that welcomes the children, affirms the strength of the community, and warms them up for the day ahead. Once the morning meeting is completed, the children move the furniture back. At the end of the day, they repeat the process.

**Use a space outside the classroom.**

Go to the cafeteria, library, gym, or other space in the school that's large enough to accommodate a circle. This solution, admittedly the most challenging, works best when you:

- **Use the same space every day.** The familiarity will help children succeed.

- **Limit distractions.** For example, if you use the cafeteria, meet when no other class is there.

- **Meet at the same time every day.** Even if it's not the most ideal time, the predictability will help students focus and feel secure.

- **Teach the expected behaviors.** Be sure to teach transition routines and behavioral expectations outside the classroom.

The whole-group meeting circle is the heart of classroom life. Sitting in a circle, everyone can see and be seen by everyone else. And because the circle has no beginning and no end, it allows everyone an equal place in the group. By the very nature of its design, the meeting circle invites group participation and fosters inclusion. Its presence and prominence in the classroom or in the school day, even if only temporary, say "In this classroom, we value working together, and we value each individual's contributions to the group."

The circle is so crucial that I recommend starting your classroom design there. Key considerations:

- **Allow enough space to have an even circle.** Find a space large enough for all of the children to sit comfortably in an even circle (not an oval, which can subtly imply that certain spots are better than others, or an amoeba, which obscures some children from view). Remember you'll also need to fit in a chart stand and other supplies for whole-group instruction.

- **Assign seats.** Once you map out the circle space, assign seats in the circle. To help the children know exactly where to sit, use tape, carpet squares, name tags, or small index cards to mark each child's spot.

16

**Three Pieces of Furniture You Can Lose**

- **A teacher's desk.** These often take up a great deal of space, but we seldom use them to teach. They tend to become places to store things and sit at the end of the day. When I got rid of my desk, I had many more options for arranging the classroom and collected much less clutter.

- **A large file cabinet.** These eat up space, too, and encourage us to keep things we don't need. Think smaller. What files are truly essential? You can probably store these in one or two small mobile file cabinets.

- **The latest, greatest thing.** Education has fads, and furniture is no exception. My first year of teaching, I paid too much for a nifty folding table to house the listening center. The table never really worked and always seemed to be in the way. You're better off sticking to the basics.

- **Rotate seat assignments.** Changing seating every week or two stretches the children to interact with many classmates, not just their preferred friend of the moment. Of course, remember to let these stability-craving children know when you're getting ready to change their spots so they can prepare mentally.

- **Move children as needed.** For instance, you may observe that a particular child is having a bad day and may need to be a little closer to you for quick reassurance or reminders. Or you may see two friends who need to be united with or separated from another friend.

- **Try free seating later in the year.** After you've taught and guided the children in practicing the skill of choosing their own spots, try shifting some seat selection responsibility to them. For much of the second grade year, however, be ready to guide and even to go back to assigning seats for awhile.

## Desk Seating

Although the circle should be your primary teaching space, students also need desks and other areas at which to do their independent and cooperative group work.

- **Try pairs if you have the space.** Second graders generally prefer to work alone or with one other person, so setting up desks in pairs is ideal.

- **Try groups if space is tight.** If you have a small room, group more desks together or use tables, but give students at least a semblance of the privacy and quiet they often crave. One cheap way to give privacy is to make a trifold barrier by gluing two file folders together. You can also use tri-fold project boards available at office supply stores.

- **Avoid the continuous U-shape.** Although a U-shaped arrangement with desks around the end of the classroom is easy, saves space, and may even suit third graders, who tend to be more gregarious and outgoing, it can feel overwhelming to most second graders.

- **Offer alternate work spaces.** Consider places other than desks where privacy-oriented second graders can work independently and productively. In my classrooms, students have liked to work under tables, on the floor in corners of the room, or in between bookshelves. Although to adults such areas may seem confining, some second graders thrive in these areas so long as they have supplies like clipboards or lap desks.

■ **Assign desk seats.** Second graders need this reassurance just as they need the reassurance of assigned seats in the circle. When assigning desks, think about (1) balancing the number of boys and girls, if possible; (2) making sure all students eventually sit with everyone in the class; (3) grouping students who have been working well together lately; (4) joining those who need a little extra help at work time with those who can help without being distracted from their own work; and (5) grouping children who need lots of quiet.

■ **Pace seating changes.** If students have alternative places to work besides their desks, you can change their desk assignments less frequently than their circle spots, about once every three to five weeks.

### Finishing Touches

Students will spend a great deal of time in their classroom, so consider adding some special but low-cost and easy-to-get items that will give the room a warm, comfortable feeling. For example:

■ **Plants** instantly brighten up a classroom. (Get low-maintenance plants.)

■ **A lamp or two** can make a reading corner cozy.

■ **Brightly colored throw pillows or bean bags** can create comforting havens for second graders when they're suffering from their frequent aches and pains.

■ **Area rugs** can help even a small classroom feel as if it has multiple areas, a huge benefit for second graders, who often need a chance to "get away from it all."

## Other Areas of the Classroom

■ **A table for meeting with small groups.** Tables come in many shapes. All you need is a simple spot where you can work with students comfortably on reading, writing, and so forth.

■ **A classroom library.** Try to provide a wide collection of books at many levels. To make browsing easier, have baskets or some other way of storing books front-facing, so children see their covers rather than their spines. (See the box "What Kinds of Books Should I Provide?" on page 19 for more on classroom books.)

■ **Accessible storage.** Math, social studies, science, and art supplies that students can use independently need to be easily accessible to all children.

■ **Private storage.** Save some space that's not accessible to the children for materials for math, social studies, science, or art (such as glitter, paint, and fancy paper) that you make available only on special occasions.

### What Kinds of Books Should I Provide?

"There are no books I can read here!" is a common complaint among second graders, who are often anxious about their reading abilities. Whether this complaint is valid or not, you *will* likely have a wide range of reading abilities, interests, and confidence levels in your classroom. So it's important to stock your classroom library with a wide variety of books. Here are some categories to consider. (For some suggested titles, see the appendix.)

■ Picture books from simple to complex

■ Chapter books from beginning level to a bit more advanced

■ Series books (second graders love these!)

■ Poetry collections

■ Joke and riddle books

■ Simple comic books

■ Nonfiction books about animals, rocks, the way things work, famous people, etc.

■ Children's magazines

■ Pop-up books

■ Mad Libs

■ Word-based books—dictionaries, pun books, complex alphabet books

# Classroom Supplies

Second graders enjoy working on projects and assignments and take great care to produce interesting, detailed, and thoughtful work. So they need a range of writing utensils, art supplies, and paper. By choosing supplies broadly and carefully, we can enliven their school experience and help them live up to their creative potential.

## Have Community Supplies Only

Rather than having students bring in their own supplies, you might want to try having classroom supplies that all students share. This gives students a sense that the classroom belongs to everyone, cuts down on competitiveness and one-upmanship, and ensures that all children have exactly what they need to succeed at school.

Community supplies may be a new concept to some parents, so be sure to take the time to explain your reasons for using them. For instance, you may want to send a note home early in the year to let parents know that community supplies help foster a sense of togetherness, ensure that all children have what they need, and cut down on competitiveness among students, which can be an issue with individual supplies.

### No Budget for Supplies?

If your school does not give you a supply budget but instead relies on parents to provide supplies, you could replace the traditional shopping list with assignments so that each parent donates one category to the class. For example, one parent supplies the pencils, another some markers, and so forth.

Also, you could explore using a website set up to link interested donors with classrooms:

- WWW.DONORSCHOOSE.ORG
- WWW.ADOPTACLASSROOM.ORG

## What Supplies Do They Need?

Walking into a teacher supply store or opening a school catalog can be overwhelming, and if you're like me, you often end up impulsively buying things students don't really need. Instead, start with the following chart of essential supplies for a second grade classroom. Although the list looks long, you'll only need to get many of the supplies once.

# Good Supplies for a Second Grade Classroom

| Category | Early in the Year | Later in the Year | Sample Quantities |
|---|---|---|---|
| **Art** | ■ Crayons<br>■ Colored pencils<br>■ Markers (thin and thick)<br>■ Watercolors<br>■ Drawing paper<br>■ Construction paper<br>■ Magazines for cutting from and other paper scraps<br>■ Brown paper bags<br>■ Found objects (buttons, fabric, cotton balls, etc.)<br>■ Scissors<br>■ Glue sticks<br>■ Glue<br>■ Tape | ■ Oil pastels<br>■ Paint<br>■ Stencils<br>■ Modeling clay<br>■ Colored tissue paper<br>■ Chenille sticks<br>■ Yarn<br>■ Glitter<br>■ Toothpicks<br>■ Wooden craft sticks | ■ Scissors—one pair for every student<br>■ Glue sticks—two per student<br>■ Glue—one bottle for every two students<br>■ Markers, crayons, colored pencils—an ample supply for each table or desk cluster<br>■ Yarn, glitter, other specialty supplies—bring out less regularly; quantity depends on how many students will use these, and how often |
| **Social studies** | ■ Globe<br>■ Maps<br>■ Atlas | ■ Map puzzles<br>■ Theme-related artifacts, pictures, and posters | ■ One globe per class<br>■ Maps of different types<br>■ One atlas per class |
| **Literacy** | ■ Books (variety of genres and reading levels)<br>■ Listening center and audio books<br>■ Variety of lined paper | ■ Books (new genres and authors to replace some books as the year progresses)<br>■ Bookmaking supplies | ■ Pencils—about eight per student<br>■ Erasers—two per student<br>■ Clipboards—one per student |

21

CONTINUED

| Category | Early in the Year | Later in the Year | Sample Quantities |
|---|---|---|---|
| **Literacy** (continued) | ■ Pencils<br>■ High-quality erasers (thick rectangular ones with some softness and flexibility)<br>■ Staplers<br>■ Writing notebooks, journals, or folders<br>■ Clipboards | | |
| **Math** | ■ Unifix cubes<br>■ Pattern blocks<br>■ Rulers<br>■ Calculators<br>■ Variety of math games<br>■ Dice<br>■ Playing/numeral cards with numbers from 1–10 (or higher) | ■ Tangrams<br>■ Geoblocks<br>■ New math games<br>■ Base ten blocks | ■ Pattern blocks, Unifix cubes, etc.—several sets<br>■ Rulers and calculators—one per student<br>■ Playing/numeral cards—one set for every two students |
| **Science** | ■ Hand lenses<br>■ Small trays (ask the meat department at your local grocery if you can have some for free)<br>■ Microscope<br>■ Magnets | ■ Balance scales<br>■ Containers for growing things or holding living things<br>■ Theme-related artifacts, pictures, and posters | ■ Hand lens—one for each student<br>■ Small tray—at least one per student<br>■ Microscope—one for the class<br>■ Balance scale—one for every two students |

## Good Supplies for a Second Grade Classroom CONTINUED

| Category | Early in the Year | Later in the Year | Sample Quantities |
|---|---|---|---|
| **Recess** (outdoor and indoor) | ■ Variety of balls<br>■ Hula-hoops<br>■ Jump ropes<br>■ Sidewalk chalk<br>■ Bubbles<br>■ Games<br>■ Puzzles | ■ More complex games<br>■ More complex puzzles | ■ Three to four balls per class<br>■ Four to six single jump ropes and two longer ones |

See the appendix for favorite books, board games, and websites for second graders.

## *Quality Matters*

Having quality supplies that work well is essential to second graders, who crave order, structure, and perfection. Markers need to make clear, solid lines; clay should be pliable and clean; and staplers should staple with one firm push from a second grader.

Mixing higher with lower quality supplies won't work. A student who finds a good marker among many dried-up ones will hoard the good one, and the trend will spread. A rule of thumb is to put out only the same sort of supplies that you would want to use yourself.

Second graders themselves are actually quite adept at quality control. With guidance, they can alert you when markers are dried out, glue bottles are empty, or the paper supply is running low. They can also place pencils in a specific container so that you'll know when these need sharpening.

## Storing and Organizing Supplies

Separate supplies according to how often they are used:

■ **Frequently needed.** I've found that a bin in the center of each desk grouping or table is a great place to store things students need almost every work period, like pencils, markers, colored pencils, crayons, and erasers.

■ **Occasionally needed.** Keep supplies that students need often but not every day on shelves accessible to them. I organize these supplies primarily by subject area. For example, in the writing area, I include various types of paper, tape, staplers (early in the year), and bookmaking supplies (later in the year).

■ **Replacement or special project supplies.** You'll need private storage for these items.

---

**To Erase or Not to Erase?**

Teaching second grade will require you to think about erasers. The first year I taught second grade, the students and I were all frustrated because they were using cheap pencil-tip erasers on cheap paper, so they often made holes in their work, a crisis for these perfectionist students. I tried to convince them that instead of erasing, they could just mark through mistakes. I was asking a great deal of them developmentally.

Over time, I learned that second graders can barely function without erasing. But what about the hole-in-the-paper problem? Some solutions I came upon:

■ Provide high-quality erasers instead of pencil-tip erasers. (Look for ones that are thick and rectangular, with some softness and flexibility.)

■ Use regular 20-pound paper—the kind you'd use to print computer documents—instead of cheap newsprint.

■ Take time to teach students how to erase properly. (See "Interactive Modeling" in Chapter 2, "Schedules and Routines," for an example of the basic steps for teaching a skill.)

## Teaching Students How to Access Supplies

I was in a second grade classroom recently where a student was sitting idle at writing time. When I asked him why, he said his pencil lead had broken, and he wasn't sure where to get another pencil.

You can avoid this kind of dilemma, typical for many second graders, by organizing supplies in a way that's easy for students to navigate and then teaching them about that organization. Label all containers—for math manipulatives, art supplies, writing utensils—and then label the shelves where they go. But don't assume children will then automatically notice these labels. I made that mistake myself for many years and was puzzled and annoyed that although I had clearly marked a shelf with "Pencils," students didn't know to go there to retrieve pencils, and although I'd marked a shelf with "Unifix Cubes," the cubes container often did not return to that spot. Once I started teaching children about the labels, most of the time they independently got the supplies they needed and put items back where they belonged.

Be explicit in teaching second graders what supplies are available in the room, when they can use them, where the supplies go, and how to care for them. Interactive Modeling is a great technique for this teaching.

**Interactive Modeling**

See Chapter 2, "Schedules and Routines," for a full explanation of Interactive Modeling.

## Making Supplies Last

If you put out all the paper you have, students will naturally look at that stack, think, "We have plenty," and go through it at an alarming rate. Instead, put out just enough paper, pencils, markers, and other supplies to last for a few months. To lessen their anxiety, let students know that you'll replenish the supplies when they run out and teach them what to do if an item has run out before you've had a chance to replenish it.

It's also important to encourage second graders to use a smaller-sized scrap of paper for a small project, rather than taking a whole sheet and using just one tiny corner.

# Classroom Displays

## *Two Guiding Principles*

■ **Less is more.** Covering every possible space with displays will make the room seem cluttered and overstimulating, especially for second graders, who have difficulty seeing objects from afar anyway. Leave much of the walls and tops of shelves clear, and leave ample borders around bulletin boards.

■ **Make displays purposeful.** Often we teachers hang up every piece of work students do, design adorable but not very meaningful bulletin boards, or leave up work that students did months ago. But students often ignore or quickly forget about these displays that we think are so wonderful, and they don't care about work they did months ago. Before you put anything up, be clear about why you're doing it and how long you're going to leave it up.

## *Student Work Should Dominate*

Many types of charts, references, and pictures are worth displaying in a classroom, but the most important thing to display is students' work. Students love to see their classmates' creations as well as their own. Displaying such work lets students know that what they do at school is important and that the classroom belongs to everyone, not just the teacher. Seeing others' work can also inspire students for future projects. In displaying student work, remember to:

■ **Include everyone.** Display work from each of the children, not just the "best" students.

■ **Display finished and draft work.** Showing in-progress work (with some cross-outs), not just end products, helps second graders recognize that perfection is not always

the goal and that everyone has areas in which to grow.

- ■ **Give students a say.** Second graders tend to be sensitive and may not be comfortable with showing a piece even if you believe it is worthy. Consider creating a display square for each student and letting each student decide what gets displayed in his or her space. Or just be sure to check with students before hanging something of theirs. Giving students a say in what is displayed has the added benefit that the displays will vary from student to student, which conveys that we value students as individuals.

- ■ **Plan for three-dimensional displays.** You can use the tops of bookshelves and countertops for these. If you just can't find the space for three-dimensional displays, or if a student's three-dimensional work includes classroom materials (like pattern blocks) that others will need soon, take a photo of the work and display that.

**Put It at Eye Level**

Whenever possible, put displays at the children's eye level. Remember that second graders have trouble seeing things far away. They'll quickly become frustrated by— or learn to ignore—displays high up on a wall.

## *Other Displays*

- ■ **Year-long references and fun charts.** Classroom rules should be up all year so you and the children can continually refer to them. (To learn about one way to create rules *with* students so that they're invested in them, see *Teaching Self-Discipline: The Responsive Classroom Guide to Helping Students Dream, Behave, and Achieve in Elementary School,* Center for Responsive Schools, 2018.) Other possible year-long items include a calendar and weather graph, a birthday graph, and a chart of lost teeth (second graders have fun keeping track of these major life changes among their class members).

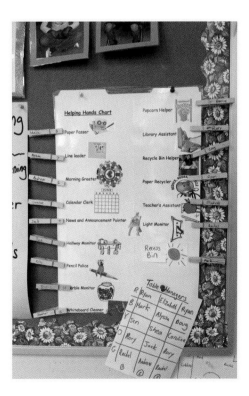

■ **Current teaching tools or content.** You may occasionally want to show charts or other reference information to go with what students are currently learning in literacy, social studies, and other content areas. But it's easy to overdo these—remember the principles "less is more" and "all displays should serve a purpose." Also keep in mind that second graders can only take in so much from a distance, so if they are working at their seats, they're probably not going to make much use of far-off word walls, spelling charts, or lists of writing topics. If any of these are truly necessary, consider creating desktop versions of them.

# Technology

Second graders are often quite capable with technology. Still, you'll want to handle carefully the use of technology in your classroom. We sometimes get swept up in excitement over new technology without thinking through how often our students will use a given device or application, what the benefits and drawbacks might be, and how that technology fits in with students' overall learning needs.

Guidelines for using any technology in a second grade classroom:

■ **Supervise carefully.** Keep most technology off limits when no adult can supervise. Even when students know a good deal about a given tool or device, they can make mistakes or think they know more than they do.

■ **Set boundaries on Internet use.** Know your school's policies about students' Internet usage, what blocks your school has in place, and what websites you're comfortable having students visit. Then teach these boundaries to students.

■ **Check in on computer use often.** Students can get into trouble quickly when they're using the Internet, so check on them frequently. If you're planning on working with small groups or individuals in an area away from the computers, restrict students to non-Internet activities.

Also, work with the experts in your school to ensure that every child can access the technology resources you plan to use.

## Closing Thoughts

Setting up a classroom with care and forethought will bring benefits to you and to students all year long. Second graders will appreciate a well-ordered, simple room with displays and supplies that make them feel valued and welcomed at school. And if, like me, you make mistakes, shake them off and go back to the drawing board. Like the second graders we teach, we benefit from realizing that we are not perfect and that our rooms are works in progress.

## CHAPTER 2

# Schedules and Routines

With their need for structure and stability, second graders do best when their teachers stick to a predictable schedule and lay out exactly what the children need to do to succeed at every routine activity across that schedule. These students love the consistency of a daily schedule, sometimes to the point of becoming rattled by any change to it. Once after one of my classes visited a colleague's second grade room, one student became visibly upset and pulled me aside to let me know he thought I should talk to this teacher. He had noticed that her schedule was "out of order"—among other things, she did math after morning meeting and had read-aloud at the end of the day. "Doesn't she know that read-aloud comes after quiet time and then you do math?" I explained that even though that's when we do read-aloud and math, other classes might have different schedules, and that's OK.

In this chapter, we'll look at practical ways to manage schedules and routines so that second graders will feel comfortable and capable. Attending to this important aspect of teaching will lead to a much smoother year for the children—and for you.

## Scheduling

The first step in creating a daily schedule for second graders is to consider how they learn best. The second step is to list the components of the day, and the third is to sketch out time slots for each component.

### Consider How Second Graders Learn Best

Second graders are very curious and love the opportunity to explore topics of interest to them, but they also crave the security of having routine, structure, and plenty of time to do their best work.

Some specifics to keep in mind:

■ **Active learning.** Second graders need to be active throughout the day. They need to get up and move often. They need to get their hands on real objects—working with manipulatives in math, for instance. They need many chances and ways to process new information. For example, if you teach a mini-lesson on a historical period, also plan for students to read about and see visuals of the period, draw or write about what they've learned, or discuss the lesson with a classmate.

■ **Interactive learning.** We all learn best when we have time to process information by communicating with others. Because second graders frequently have trouble imagining different perspectives and can get stuck in their own thinking, opportunities to talk with others about their learning are particularly helpful for them.

32

■ **Changes of pace and place.** Second graders do best when the pace of their day is varied and they're not physically stuck in one place all day. If you have a fairly long and quiet writing period planned, move students back to the circle for a closing reflection. Then do a quick game or interactive mini-lesson before moving everyone back to their tables to begin your next teaching block.

### What About Pacing Guides?

Many schools require teachers to follow pacing or time guides. Of course, you'll need to adhere to these as closely as you can, but try not to lose sight of the children's needs in the process. If your district requires ninety minutes of language arts instruction, for example, working some quick movement, talking, hands-on work, or reflection breaks into that ninety minutes will refresh the children and help ease any tension they may be feeling. For lively movement breaks that take just one to three minutes, see *Energizers! 88 Quick Movement Activities That Refresh and Refocus* by Susan Lattanzi Roser (Center for Responsive Schools, 2009). Other resources are listed in Chapter 4, "Classroom Games, Special Projects, and Field Trips."

■ **Energy levels.** As a general rule, second graders have more energy in the mornings than the afternoons. So schedule work that's mentally more challenging for them—such as reading and writing—earlier in the day.

Even with their energy in the morning, they'll still need you to break up their intense reading and writing work with movement breaks, read-alouds, shared reading, time to turn and talk, or hands-on language arts work such as art, drama, or games focused on the language arts curriculum.

Keep things active in the afternoons as well. Math, science, social studies, and word work can all be structured in ways that get students up and moving around.

■ **Need for food.** To stay alert all morning—especially when they're scheduled for late lunch—second graders typically need additional sustenance, so it's important to schedule time for them to have a morning snack.

## List the Day's Components

List both the academic and social components of an average day. Here's a list I've found to be a good starting place:

| | |
|---|---|
| Morning meeting | Word study/spelling |
| Shared reading | Math |
| Reading workshop | Science |
| Chapter book read-aloud | Social studies |
| Writing workshop | Closing routines |

## Order the Day

Second graders love the consistency a predictable schedule brings, so you'll want to plan the day carefully. Even though some components of the day (such as lunch and specials) may fall into fixed slots that you can't change, it's still worthwhile to sketch out an ideal schedule based on second graders' needs and then adjust it as necessary. Doing so will help keep your scheduling child-centered. Here are a couple of ideal schedules you can work from.

| | |
|---|---|
| 7:45–8:00 | Arrival routine |
| 8:00–8:30 | Morning meeting |
| 8:30–8:50 | Word work |
| 8:50–9:10 | Shared reading and reading mini-lesson |
| 9:10–10:00 | Reading workshop, including picture book read-aloud |
| 10:00–10:15 | Snack (can be combined with quiet reading, listening to jokes/poems, catch-up time) |
| 10:15–11:00 | Writing workshop |
| 11:00–11:30 | Special |
| 11:30–12:00 | Recess . . . free play |
| 12:00–12:30 | Lunch |
| 12:30–12:50 | Quiet time |
| 12:50–1:50 | Math |
| 1:50–2:05 | Read-aloud |
| 2:05–2:45 | Science/social studies |
| 2:45–2:50 | Clean up and pack |
| 2:50–3:00 | Closing circle (see "Dismissal Routines" on page 49) |
| 3:00 | Dismissal |

| | |
|---|---|
| 7:45–8:00 | Arrival routine |
| 8:00–8:30 | Morning meeting |
| 8:30–9:15 | Writing workshop |
| 9:15–9:30 | Snack |
| 9:30–9:50 | Shared reading and reading mini-lesson |
| 9:50–10:40 | Reading workshop, including picture book read-aloud |
| 10:40–11:40 | Math |
| 11:40–12:10 | Recess . . . free play |
| 12:10–12:40 | Lunch |
| 12:40–1:00 | Quiet time |
| 1:00–1:40 | Science/social studies |
| 1:40–2:00 | Read-aloud |
| 2:00–2:30 | Special |
| 2:30–2:50 | Word work |
| 2:50–2:55 | Clean up and pack |
| 2:55–3:00 | Closing circle (see "Dismissal Routines" on page 49) |
| 3:00 | Dismissal |

34

### Give Movement Breaks Often!

Regardless of what schedule you come up with, insert movement breaks throughout the day as the children need them.

# Teaching Classroom Routines

When I started teaching, I was surprised that students didn't come to school knowing how to do tasks I thought were routine, such as sharpening pencils, asking for my attention, or taking out and putting away drawing materials. On reflection, though, I realized that younger children may never have done some of these tasks. Even if they had, I probably expected the tasks to be done differently. I realized that I would have to help each class feel safe, secure, and happy by teaching them how I wanted classroom routines to look and sound.

## *Use Interactive Modeling to Teach Routines*

One effective way to teach classroom routines is through Interactive Modeling. This teaching practice breaks routines down into small parts and gives students multiple opportunities to observe, discuss, and try each behavior or skill. Once you get the structure down, you'll find that Interactive Modeling goes pretty quickly. Plus, the time and effort you put into modeling routines early in the year will pay off in reduced misbehavior, smoother transitions, and more time for learning all year long.

The next page shows what the steps of Interactive Modeling might sound and look like if you were teaching students how to sit in a circle and focus on the teacher.

# Interactive Modeling—Sitting Safely and Focusing on the Teacher

| Steps to Follow | Might Sound and Look Like |
|---|---|
| Say what you will model and why. | "When you sit on the rug, it's important that you be safe and that you focus. Watch while I show you how to sit safely and focus on the teacher." |
| Model the behavior. | Designate a student as the pretend teacher. Sit safely and direct your focus to the student. Remain quiet. You do not need to narrate as you model. |
| Ask students what they noticed. | "What did you notice about how I sat and focused?" (If necessary, follow up with questions such as "What did you notice my hands doing?" or "What were my eyes doing?" to prompt children to list the important elements: kept hands and feet to yourself, looked at teacher, remained quiet, etc.) |
| Invite one or more students to model. | "Who can show us how to sit on the rug and focus the same way I did?" |
| Again, ask students what they noticed. | "How did Noah show he was focusing on me when I was speaking?" The children name Noah's specific safe and focused behaviors. |
| Have all students practice. | "Now we're all going to practice sitting safely and focusing. I'll be watching and seeing you do all the things we just practiced." |
| Provide feedback. | "You did it! You all sat with your legs, arms, and hands in your own space. Your eyes were on me when I talked, and you were leaning forward a little, just to show that extra bit of attention." |

## Keys to Successful Interactive Modeling

BE CLEAR ABOUT HOW YOU WANT THINGS DONE

Rather than just saying "sit safely and respectfully in the circle," show students exactly what the acceptable ways to sit are (I recommend cross-legged or on their knees). Rather than simply telling children they can talk in the hall with quiet voices, show them what a quiet voice sounds like. Detail-oriented second graders will pay attention to how you model a routine the first time, so think through each step before modeling.

### More Benefits of Interactive Modeling

Students . . .

- Become better observers (a skill that transfers into their academic work)

- Begin to value each other as models

- Become more engaged in monitoring their own behavior

USE A SCRIPT

Having a basic script handy will help you to be exact in your modeling—and to refrain from talking too much! Using fewer words helps your students concentrate on essentials and also allows more time for them to practice and observe.

KEEP EXPECTATIONS HIGH

Once you've modeled and practiced a routine, make sure students meet the expectations you've established. That will keep the classroom orderly and the children secure. If you say that when you raise your hand, students should finish their sentence and look at you, don't start giving directions while most but not all students are ready. Doing so signals that you don't really mean what you say, which can make second graders feel very uncomfortable and unsafe.

**Making Adjustments for Particular Students**

Although it's good to have high expectations for all children, invariably you'll encounter students for whom those expectations are unrealistic. Perhaps you generally expect students to sit empty-handed while in the circle, but you may have a student who needs to hold a certain object to stay calm and focused. Be prepared to adjust your expectations as necessary. Also be sure to discuss with your class why you might occasionally modify rules for particular students. Explain that each of us needs different things to do our best: For example, some of us need glasses; others don't. Similarly, some of us need to hold something in our hands to stay focused; most of us don't. It's the teacher's job to help figure out what each student needs.

### KEEP EXPECTATIONS APPROPRIATE

Sometimes, as we work to keep expectations high, we may ask too much of our students. Perfectionistic second graders may react with anxiety to expectations that are beyond them developmentally or simply unrealistic. For instance, a teacher might tell students they may go to the bathroom anytime except when they might miss important instruction or information. But most second graders can't distinguish what is essential from what is not. Even if they could make this distinction ordinarily, they certainly won't be able to when they need to go to the bathroom, an anxiety-provoking time for children at this age. If your students react with anxiety and confusion to a task you ask them to do, think about whether what you've asked is appropriate for them and if so, why they're confused. If necessary, break the task down into smaller steps, teach those steps, and always be ready to offer guidance and support. See, for example, "Bathroom Routines" on page 42.

### GIVE STUDENTS PLENTY OF PRACTICE

We often expect students to "get it right" the first time they try a new behavior. But just as with academic subjects such as reading or math, children need time to practice behavioral skills. Give them several opportunities to practice and "mess up" with a new behavior, and keep these practice sessions fun and

light. For instance, when practicing how to participate in a group discussion, make a hash mark on chart paper each time children remember to raise their hands before speaking. If someone messes up during practice, simply treat this as a mistake, not a tragedy, just as you would if a student misread a word in a new text or made an addition error. Simply say, "Oops, you forgot to raise your hand. Try again."

### REINFORCE SUCCESS OFTEN

Second graders thrive on positive feedback and need you to pay attention to things they're doing well: "I noticed that you all kept your hands to yourselves and had quiet voices on the way to the library." "I see that you all remembered how to carry your chairs safely to morning meeting." Pay particular attention to struggling students and find a private moment with those children to reinforce their successes even more often. Hearing about what they're doing well shows these students that even though following the rules is hard for them, you see and appreciate that they're trying.

**When to Reteach Routines**

Here are a few times when students will benefit from extra attention to routines:

- Monday morning
- Friday afternoon
- Right after vacation
- Before and after you've had a substitute teacher
- Around the holidays
- When a new student joins the class
- Before assemblies and field trips

39

## Key Routines to Teach

At the beginning of the year, teach those routines that will most concern your students and those that will get your classroom up and running quickly and efficiently. Here are the most important routines to focus on.

### RESPONDING TO SIGNALS FOR ATTENTION

When I was student teaching, one professor said he could tell if a teacher had good management skills by watching whether she could get her students' attention whenever she needed it. This lesson stuck with me, and once I had my own classroom, the first thing I always modeled was how students should respond to my signals for attention.

Using a signal is more respectful than calling out "Hey, kids" or "Listen up" or beginning to give directions before children are ready. Signals are also more effective than too much teacher talk ("Okay, everyone, it's time to come to the circle for reading. Owen, I need you to listen when I'm giving directions. Vivi and Matthew, stop doing that and clean up. Everyone needs to be heading this way to the circle. I'm about to read a book to you. Don't you want to hear it?"). After the first few words, students will tend to tune out your voice. Using a signal also has a calming effect so that students become quiet and more ready to listen. Further, when taught and used correctly, the signal gives students the message that we expect all of them, not just some, to listen and learn.

Whatever signals you use, it's respectful and realistic to give children a few seconds to finish what they're saying or doing before expecting them to be quiet and attentive. Second graders especially become very involved in whatever they're doing and find it hard to stop immediately.

In general, I use two kinds of signals: visual and auditory.

■ **Visual signal.** Simply raising your hand is a good way to signal for the attention of children working with you in a circle or at a table. When children see your hand raised, they quickly finish what they're saying or doing, raise one hand to help spread the signal, put their other hand in their lap, and look at you.

■ **Auditory signal.** When students are spread out around the room working, an auditory signal such as a wind chime, rain stick, or other pleasant-sounding instrument works well. When they hear the sound, children moving about the room freeze and look at you. Children working at their desks quickly finish the word they're writing or the sentence they're saying and look at you.

**Having a Substitute Teacher?**
**Keep the Schedule and Key Routines in Place!**

**Schedules.** It may be tempting to plan something different to make the day with the substitute, or "guest teacher," feel more special. But in this situation, different feels worse to routine-oriented second graders.

**Routines.** Be specific in your lessons plans about any special routines or traditions the class has. For instance, if you typically begin math with a warm-up activity, choose an easy one for the guest teacher, but do not have her skip it.

**Other ways to help the day go smoothly.**

■ Choose several students the guest teacher can ask about the schedule and routines (rotate among students over the course of the year).

■ Discuss with the class ways they can care for each other and the guest teacher while you're out (do what the guest teacher says even if it's different from what you would do, remember that you'll be back tomorrow, etc.) Leave these ideas for the guest teacher to review with the class.

■ Interactively model and practice being with a guest teacher. For example, have a colleague, pretending to be the guest teacher, act out doing spelling activities in the wrong order. Model and then let students practice how to do the activities in that order or how to respectfully let her know the correct order.

Of course, students will also need to gain your attention, so teach them how to do so appropriately. Two signals will be helpful when you are working with the whole group.

■ **Raising a hand.** If a student wants to tell you something in the ordinary course of a discussion, raising a hand works. But be sure to model and practice waiting until a classmate has finished speaking before raising a hand. When students have their hands raised, they're often thinking ahead to what they're going to say rather than listening, so we need to teach them strategies to help them listen fully to others.

■ **SOS for emergencies.** For emergencies (bloody nose, feeling sick, and so forth), have a separate signal like SOS (hand shut, hand open, hand shut). Because second graders have frequent aches and pains, be sure to cover in detail what constitutes an emergency and privately help students who struggle with these distinctions as the year goes on.

### BATHROOM ROUTINES

Second graders worry considerably about having bathroom accidents, so you'll need to teach bathroom routines as soon as possible—preferably on the first day of school. Your routine may well depend upon where the bathrooms are located, but if possible, second graders need to be able to go to the bathroom "as needed," rather than having to wait for appointed times.

I usually allow one student at a time (of each gender) to go to the bathroom. They simply go to a pocket chart that contains cards with their names, remove their card, and put it in the bathroom slot. When they return, they put their card back in the pocket chart.

Other things to model and practice are how much toilet paper to use, how to wash hands thoroughly, and how to wipe around the sinks.

### Who Goes First?

No matter what grade you teach, students will worry about who gets to be first in line. Second graders, who see this issue in terms of fairness, are no different, and if the same people are first each day, others will notice and object.

I often hear teachers tell students, "Don't worry about who's first—we're all going to the same place, so it doesn't matter who gets there first." This reasoning wouldn't work for me as I wait in line to board an airplane, buy things at the store, or get my driver's license. It won't convince many children, either. So think through how to handle who'll go first: Will you call students to line up by table groups or categories ("If you have blue on, line up"), or use some numeric system? It doesn't really matter what method you use, as long as you don't leave it to the children to decide who goes first.

### MORNING ROUTINES

The morning arrival period is a great time to ask about personal events or siblings, make connections, and check in with students. Students also need the sense of structure that comes from completing morning tasks. Suggestions for a productive morning routine:

■ **Manageable tasks.** Give children some basic tasks to accomplish, but avoid loading them up with too much "morning work."

■ **Pleasant environment.** Have music or an audiobook playing as the children arrive (poetry works well—anyone can enjoy it whenever they walk in).

■ **Individual activities.** If children arrive over a period of time rather than all at once, consider letting early arrivers do some quiet activities—for instance, working puzzles, playing with blocks or Legos, journaling, reading, or doing math puzzles.

### SITTING IN THE CIRCLE FOR WHOLE-GROUP LESSONS

Many of us adults are still learning how to show that we're focused and listening, so it's unrealistic to assume that children will have mastered this skill by second grade. What components of respectful listening are important to you? I generally allow students to sit cross-legged or on their knees. I expect students to focus their eyes on whoever is speaking and to keep their hands and feet close to their bodies. I also let them stand up to take a stretch break when they need to (and of course to leave for bathroom and other emergencies).

Fast and efficient transitions are key to the smooth running of any class-room, and these are especially important for second graders, who may feel unsafe when they have too much unstructured, unguided time. You'll need to teach students ways to quickly transition from one activity to another in your classroom and from your classroom to other locations in the school. To avoid losing important time for instruction, lunch, or play, think through how students can make efficient transitions, teach them how to do that, and practice those skills until they are proficient with them.

Transitions into and outside of the classroom:

■ **Leave enough time to shift gears calmly.** Students will handle hallways and whatever their next activity is more successfully if they have a chance to become calm, come together as a community, and think ahead to what's next. Rather than rushing your students out the door, leave enough time to call them to line up calmly, ask them to close their eyes and take a deep breath, or play a quick but quiet game like a silent follow-the-teacher. You might also consider playing some quiet, soft music as students leave the room.

■ **Model lining up and walking in hallways.** The more time you devote to modeling and having students practice routines for getting from one

44

### How to Teach Line and Hallway Routines

■ **Decide where the line should be.** Where should children line up in the classroom before they leave? Choose a spot with few distractions where all the students can comfortably stand in a line.

■ **Teach exactly how to line up.** Model and have students practice walking quickly to the line without stopping to touch or look at anything on the way, facing front, keeping arms at their sides, and leaving space between people (I show students a distance of elbow to fingertips when I model lining up, and they come up with their own way of describing this distance).

■ **Teach expected hallway behavior.** If you have a choice, allow children to talk quietly as they walk, as this is more appropriate for second graders. But be sure to model and have students practice exactly what volume is OK. Otherwise, you may end up spending too much time turning down the volume. I also model and have students practice walking at a steady pace and staying together (by maintaining that elbow-to-fingertip distance).

■ **Walk with your class.** Second graders are not ready for the responsibility of walking as a class without their teacher. They will feel unsafe doing so.

place to another safely and efficiently, the safer and more secure they'll feel, and the fewer "line incidents" you'll have. See the box above for a good way to approach this teaching.

■ Spell out what to do upon arriving back in the classroom. Think through exactly where you want students to be and what you want them to do before they enter the classroom, and spell these expectations out to them. ("When we get to the classroom, go to your spot in the circle, sit quietly, and wait for our read-aloud. It's a good one today!") Stop the line right at your classroom door and remind everyone of the expectations (or have a student or two do the reminding).

Transitions within the classroom:

■ Model how to move from the circle to desks. You can save a great deal of instructional time by making transitions from the circle to desks smooth and seamless. Model and practice how it looks and sounds for children to leave the circle, get necessary materials, go back to their desks, and quickly get to work on a project or assignment. Depending upon what they need to do to get ready for an assignment, most second graders should be able to get back to their seats and be ready to work in only a few minutes.

■ **Model how to move from desks to the circle.** Just as explicitly, you'll need to model how it looks and sounds to stop working, clean up, and come back to the circle. Be sure to teach students where to put materials, what they should do with both finished and unfinished work, and how long cleaning up should take. It often helps to have a specific song that you play as students clean up—when the song ends, they should be in place in the circle.

INDEPENDENT WORK-TIME ROUTINES

Establishing productive and efficient independent work times will take several weeks for second graders. As you think through what you want work times to look and sound like, consider the children's developmental needs as well as your own tolerance for noise and movement. Some key considerations:

■ **Work place.** If at all possible, let second graders work on the floor, in any private little corners or areas you can set up, and even under tables or desks. They enjoy these confined spaces.

■ **Changing places.** Second graders can sustain their attention to work for increasingly longer periods (but usually no more than thirty minutes) once there's a sense of calm in the room, with few students up and moving. It's best, therefore, to teach children to stay in the place they've chosen once they begin working.

■ **Work posture.** Most second graders prefer to sit and work, but some may work better standing. Let them do so, as long as they can be productive.

■ **Getting your attention.**
Many second graders bene-
fit from frequent check-ins
with their teacher. Try
teaching students to seek
help from friends if they
are "stuck" and to work
on an alternate assignment
if their friends can't help.
Then, leave whatever group
or individual with whom
you're working every fifteen
minutes or so for a brief check-in around the room with students working
independently. For emergencies, teach students to come to you, tap your
shoulder, and show you the "SOS" sign.

READ-ALOUD ROUTINES

Second graders often respond to read-alouds with uninhibited emotions.
My class begged, "Can you read just one more chapter, please?" every day
when I was reading Lois Lowry's *Gooney Bird Greene*. "Read it again!" someone might cry when I read the deceptively simple picture book *Don't Let the
Pigeon Drive the Bus* by Mo Willems. Sometimes their mesmerized silence
would say it all, as when we read *The Man Who Walked Between the Towers*
by Mordicai Gerstein.

Second graders enjoy funny and serious selections, true-to-life stories,
mysteries and fantasies, and any book with strong and interesting characters. In many ways, it's a smorgasbord year, with the children needing
(and loving) to try out many different types of books as they begin to
develop their reading tastes.

Focus on the specific needs of second graders to make the most of read-
aloud time:

■ **Try to read aloud several times each day.** Vary your selections among
picture books, chapter books, and portions of nonfiction books (perhaps
related to your science or social studies theme or to a math topic). You
might create a selection of joke and poetry books from which to read

aloud when you have an extra moment in the circle or while lining up. Some of these read-alouds can be as short as a few minutes.

■ **Schedule effectively.** Remember second graders' need to balance more active times with more quiet times. Let this be your guide in scheduling read-alouds. For example, read-alouds work especially well after an active time like P.E. or recess.

■ **Scaffold for success.** Second graders can develop quite lengthy attention spans, but they need to do so gradually. At the beginning of the year, choose shorter, simpler selections—for example, picture books that you can read in five to ten minutes and chapter books with similarly short chapters. As the year progresses, gradually add longer and more complex texts.

■ **Keep the room focused and quiet.** In general, second graders do not need to draw, get up and move around, eat snacks, or do anything else besides listen during read-alouds. In fact, most of them need a calm and quiet classroom to fully enjoy the read-aloud experience. You will, of course, want to accommodate any students who struggle with attention. Depending on the child, you might let him or her draw, squeeze a squeeze toy, or, upon a signal from you, get up and move about for a few minutes.

Occasionally, second graders have bathroom accidents, vomit, throw temper tantrums, have bloody noses, or become caught up in some other crisis that requires your full attention. At these times, it's crucial for the rest of the class to know what you expect them to do while you're helping the child who's having trouble. I teach students that when I say, "This is an emergency time," they should take these steps:

- **Students keep working.** If they're working independently, just keep working.

- **Students read at their seats.** If they're meeting in the circle, return to their desks, pull out a book, and start reading.

> **Remember to Teach Recess and Lunch Routines!**
>
> See Chapter 3, "Building Community," to learn more about those middle-of-the-day routines.

Practice this routine until the class has it down pat. It'll help you deal with those occasional emergencies more efficiently, and it'll help all the children feel safe.

## DISMISSAL ROUTINES

Second graders are typically pretty spent by dismissal time and can't keep in mind a long list of end-of-the-day tasks. If you expect them to straighten their desks, put homework in their folders, get their backpacks and coats,

put their folders and other materials in their backpacks, and remember how to get to buses, cars, or parents quickly and safely, you'll be setting them up for frustration. As with all "to do" lists for second graders, keep the dismissal list as short as possible. See if some tasks can be done more successfully earlier in the day, such as putting homework in folders and straightening their desks.

Before dismissal, try to carve out time for a brief but meaningful close to the day in the form of a closing circle. During this time, you might want to engage children in some quick reflection about the day ("What are some things that went well for you?" or "What are some ways we took care of each other today?") You may also want to choose one or two aspects about the upcoming day to highlight. Finally, you may want to end with a familiar song, chant, or cheer. Sending second graders home on a positive note makes them feel more confident and secure and leaves them looking forward to their return to school.

### OTHER ROUTINES

Some other routines and social skills you may want to model and practice:

- Indoor recess routines

- Taking care of and putting away class supplies

- Winning and losing a game graciously

- Fire, earthquake, or tornado drill routines

- Greeting former teachers, friends, and family when children see them around the school

- Completing class jobs

- Turning in homework

- Closing circle

**Learn More About Schedules and Routines**

*The First Six Weeks of School,* 2nd ed. (Center for Responsive Schools, 2015).

## Closing Thoughts

By creating and sticking to a predictable schedule that fits second graders' needs, you can give them a good measure of the safety and security they crave. Taking time to think through and explicitly teach classroom routines and behaviors further adds to children's sense of comfort and stability. The time you invest in this work will make for a more comfortable and productive year for everyone.

## CHAPTER 3

# Building Community

Like all children, second graders learn best when they feel safely connected to their teachers and classmates. In a safe classroom community, all children feel known, cared for, appreciated, and important to the group. When we help children create such a community, we free them to be playful and to take risks—both essential conditions for learning.

The power and influence of that sense of community reveal themselves in both small and large moments. Not long ago, I had a class in which several students struggled with social skills. As the school year began, these students always seemed to be alone on the playground at recess time. After I guided the class through several weeks of intentional community building, I noticed many students frequently going out of their way to invite the children who were usually alone to join them in whatever they were doing. Another year, several children spontaneously made cards and notes when one of their classmates became so sick that she was going to miss school for more than a week. And the year a student in our school died, I remember how my students just wanted to be with each other that day and clearly drew support from their closeness in a difficult time.

In this chapter, we'll explore ways to nurture the kind of caring, thoughtful community that will enable second graders to grow and thrive all year long.

## Teacher Tone and Demeanor

Classroom community building begins with us teachers. In our first encounter with students, in each interaction in the days that follow, and throughout the year, we can use our tone, demeanor, and choice of words to tell students that we value having a safe, respectful community and that we want them to value it, too. Specific ways to convey that message:

- **Speak to all children in the same caring way.** By speaking to each of your students with kindness, respect, and a sense of friendly curiosity about them as people, you model for the class how you want them to speak to each other.

- **Show by example how to treat others kindly.** To help your second graders feel secure and to create a climate of respect, you need to show them what kind behavior looks like. For instance, when a child makes a mistake in front of the class, model a gentle, understanding response like "That's OK—mistakes help us learn. Just try again."

- **Recognize positives in the whole class.** By doing so, you help children understand that they're a team with common struggles and strengths: "Wow, we all lined up for recess in less than a minute—we're really taking care of each other's time."

- **Recognize challenges in a matter-of-fact way.** Give children opportunities and ideas for how to work together toward improvement: "I've noticed that we've had trouble cleaning up and coming to the circle quickly. I know it's hard to stop what you're doing, but we have important things to discuss in the circle and need everyone to be on time. What can we all do to help each other with this goal?"

- **Get to know each child as well as you can.** Your efforts, which the children will notice, will convey that everyone is valued in the classroom community. Briefly chat with students when they come in during the morning ("Hi, John, how did your baseball game go?"), give them writing assignments that will reveal their lives, likes, and interests ("You're going to write about your favorite part of school last year"), or sit and talk with them at lunch ("Your mom gave you a note in your lunchbox! How often does she do that?").

# Greetings

The first step in building community is making sure everyone knows everyone else's name. But learning names doesn't always happen naturally, especially among second graders, who are often not outgoing enough to approach classmates on their own. So in the first weeks of school, lead lots of games and activities that help children learn classmates' names.

Also make sure you greet students by name each day as they arrive. Try to begin the day in a circle with students formally greeting each other as well.

### Ideas for Learning Names

Playful ways of learning classmates' names not only make it easier for students to remember the names but also help the children bond. Just be sure that whatever idea you use honors the name that students prefer to be called by (first name? middle name? nickname?) and its proper pronunciation (seek parent help if you need to).

■ **Simple name games.** Display all the children's photos and let the class practice identifying all of their classmates. Or place name cards in the middle of your meeting circle and let students draw a name and find the matching classmate. Have fun with the children making up your own class games!

■ **Personalized name tags.** Have students decorate name tags to wear and place on their desks and cubbies so that their names are visible in several places. Depending on your students' needs, consider having them wear name tags for the first week of class.

■ **Academic activities using names.** Graph the names of everyone in the class from shortest to longest. Write all of the children's names on a chart and look for common spelling patterns, consonant blends, vowel combinations, or digraphs. Let students write poems about themselves using the letters of their names in acrostic form. The possibilities are endless.

Warm, friendly greetings from classmates and the teacher set a positive tone and let children know that their presence matters to others. Daily greetings also get students engaged with each other—especially important for second graders, who tend to be somewhat reticent socially.

Greetings can also build essential social skills, such as turning toward the person you're greeting; using a friendly, open face; speaking clearly; and shaking hands firmly but gently.

Ways to help second graders learn names and succeed with greetings:

■ Play name games. Being playful builds a sense of community while students are learning names. It can even build academic skills. See the box "Ideas for Learning Names" above.

■ Model new greetings. Modeling helps children understand exactly how the greeting should look and sound. Be sure also to model silently watching and listening while other children in the circle are exchanging greetings.

**Interactive Modeling**

See Chapter 2, "Schedules and Routines," for a full explanation of Interactive Modeling.

■ Begin with simple greetings. As the children become more comfortable with you and each other, gradually introduce more complex greetings, making sure to model them first and then giving the children plenty of practice.

# Interactive Modeling of Greetings

| Steps to Follow | Might Sound and Look Like |
|---|---|
| 1 Say what you will model and why. | "One of our class rules is 'Be friendly to everyone.' Today, each person in the class will greet someone else in a respectful and friendly way. I'm going to greet Jenny. Watch me carefully and listen to what I say." |
| 2 Model the behavior. | "Good morning, Jenny." Use a friendly tone, show a friendly face, and turn your body so you're facing Jenny. |
| 3 Ask students what they noticed. | "What did you notice about how I greeted Jenny?" (If necessary, follow up with questions such as "What kind of voice did I use?" or "What did you notice about my body?" to prompt children to list the important elements: friendly voice, friendly face, body turned to the person, used her name, etc.) |
| 4 Invite one or more students to model. | "Let's have two people volunteer to greet each other in those same ways." |
| 5 Again, ask students what they noticed. | "What did Leo and Max do to show respect and friendliness as they greeted each other?" |
| 6 Have all students practice. | "Now we're all going to practice. I'm going to partner you up, and you're going to try greeting your partner. I'll be watching and seeing you do all the things we just practiced." |
| 7 Provide feedback. | "I saw lots of people using friendly faces and voices. It sounded like many people remembered to greet their partner by name. We'll try it again tomorrow to see if we can continue starting our days in a friendly, positive way." |

# Good Greetings for Different Times of the Year

| Beginning of Year | Middle of Year | End of Year |
|---|---|---|
| Focus on the basics of greeting (turn bodies toward each other, friendly face, etc.) | Vary greetings so that students are still practicing the basics but also trying more complex greetings. | Continue with complex greetings but also include plenty of simple, heartfelt greetings as students prepare to say goodbye. |

- **Teacher greetings.** Greet students individually around the circle, modeling correct name pronunciation, appropriate voice and facial expression, etc.

- **Around-the-circle simple greetings.** Pass a friendly "good morning" or "hello" around the circle with no handshake or other body contact.

- **Greeting assigned partners.** Have students pull names from a bag. Or make pairs of numbered cards (two 1s, two 2s, etc.) and have students draw cards. Children with the same number greet each other.

- **Physical greetings.** Use handshakes, high fives, or fist bumps.

- **More playful greetings.** Greet a classmate and then toss the person a soft ball or beanbag.

- **Chants.** Greet each person with a fun, friendly chant: "1, 2, 3, 4, come on, _____, hit the floor. We're so glad you're here today. Hooray, hooray, hooray!"

- **Appreciation greetings.** "Good morning, _____, I appreciate how you've _____ this year." (Students fill in with phrases such as "helped me with math" or "played soccer so hard.")

- **Silent greetings/sign language greetings.** Express friendliness merely with facial and body language.

57

**Learn More About Greetings and Morning Meetings**

*The Morning Meeting Book*, 3rd ed., by Roxann Kriete and Carol Davis (Center for Responsive Schools, 2014).

*99 Activities and Greetings: Great for Morning Meeting . . . and Other Meetings, Too!* by Melissa Correa-Connolly (Center for Responsive Schools, 2004).

# Getting to Know Each Other

Perhaps the best and easiest way to help students get to know each other is to regularly give them time to share information about themselves. This sharing can be done in ways that are fun for students and reinforce the message that they're all important members of their class. As the children share, you'll also learn more about each of them and get an idea of their social and academic abilities.

## Topics for Sharing

Because second graders may be risk-averse and inward-looking, they'll appreciate your providing a specific topic for their sharing. A few ideas to get you started:

- Hobbies

- After-school activities

- Something you're good at doing

- Family traditions

- Life happenings—weekend fun, lost tooth stories, happy family memories, funny things that happened at home, etc.

- Favorites—foods, books, TV shows, games, sports, etc.

- Wishful thoughts—a place you'd like to visit, a time in history you'd like to go to, a book or movie whose world you'd like to enter, etc.

## Structures for Sharing

EARLY IN THE YEAR

- **Around-the-circle sharing.** After everyone speaks briefly about a topic, such as a favorite hobby, what they did on the weekend, or a book they'd like to read, encourage the children to find commonalities and connections by asking some guiding questions: "Who heard someone share a hobby similar to yours?" "Who found out that a classmate likes the same kinds of books that you do?"

- **"Introduce yourself" writing.** Students create a biography page on which they draw a picture of themselves and write key facts underneath it (name, age, siblings, pets, favorite thing to do at school, something I hope to learn this year).

- **Getting-to-know-you display.** Give each student a square on a bulletin board. Let students choose objects or draw pictures that represent their families, interests, and life so far.

LATER IN THE YEAR

- **Sharing in the circle.** Each day, one to three children share an interest or a story from home. Good topics include extracurricular activities, pets, family events, or personal accomplishments. Model and practice how to stay on topic and how much to say (stating the big idea and one or two little ideas that go with it works well). For example: "This morning my puppy chewed up my mom's new shoe. My mom got kind of mad." Also teach listeners how to look at the speaker and ask pertinent questions. For the puppy share, classmates might ask "Has the puppy chewed anything

## Keeping Sharing Safe for Everyone

Students often need our help recognizing what news is appropriate for sharing and what should be kept private or shared only with a teacher. Ideas for giving this help:

- **Brainstorm appropriate topics with students.** Post the list.

- **Give examples of private and public information.** Private: "My brother had an argument with my mom about homework." Public: "My brother and I made up a new game together."

- **Have students check with you first if they're unsure.** Tell students if they're ever unsure whether something should be shared, they should run it by you first.

- **Check in with sharers.** Consider briefly checking in with the day's scheduled sharers to find out what they're planning to share. If a topic is inappropriate, review what the class discussed about privacy and help the child find a satisfying alternative topic.

- **Enlist parents' help.** Explain the goals of sharing. Let them know that if the family has any unsettling news, they should talk with their child about sharing it only with you.

- **React calmly if a student does share something inappropriate.** This sometimes happens despite our best efforts. Stop the sharing calmly, try not to embarrass the student, and move on. For instance, "Sean, that sounds like something you and I should discuss privately. You and I will talk, and then you can share about it or something else later."

For more information about sharing, see *The Morning Meeting Book*, 3rd ed., by Roxann Kriete and Carol Davis (Center for Responsive Schools, 2014).

else?" or "What is your puppy's name?" The sharer responds before the next sharer takes his or her turn.

■ **Event narratives.** Students write in detail about a small event from their lives ("How I found a four-leaf clover this morning"). Students can also write about information they've shared orally, such as a family tradition.

■ **Poems.** Children write and share poems about things they love, find very funny, or have other strong feelings about.

### STRUCTURES FOR THE WHOLE YEAR

Many games designed to help children get to know each other work well to keep them in touch throughout the year. For example:

■ **Human Bingo.** Fill a bingo grid with statements such as "I have a dog" and "I love to draw." Students find classmates who match the statements.

■ **Just Like Me.** Students go around the circle making a statement about themselves such as "I like to play checkers." Others who also like to play checkers stand up and say "Just like me!"

■ **Musical Partners.** Play some music. When the music stops, students find a partner and answer a question you pose, such as "What's your favorite color?" Play several rounds.

See Chapter 4, "Classroom Games, Special Projects, and Field Trips," to learn more about these and other classroom games.

## Model How to Share Information

Interactive Modeling will help students succeed with sharing information with the group or a partner. Be sure to model:

■ How much information to share

■ What kind of information to share (see the box "Keeping Sharing Safe for Everyone" on page 59)

■ How loudly to speak

■ What facial and body language to use while sharing

■ What good listening looks like (occasionally nodding, turning toward the speaker, etc.)

# Class Celebrations

Celebrating the end of a unit, an author the class loves, or even a whole curricular area can foster community, spur enthusiasm for learning, and allow children to develop skills and learn concepts in a unique way. Celebrations also create special memories that students will carry with them. A favorite among the second graders I've taught is an insect museum day, when the children display for families and other classes the insects they made in art class, share their written reports, and give talks about the most interesting things they learned about their insects.

## Ideas for Celebrations

The possibilities for class celebrations are endless and will depend upon your curriculum, the guidelines and traditions of your school or team, and your resources. Nonetheless, here are a few ideas to get you started.

| Ideas for Celebrations | 61 |
| --- | --- |

| Curriculum Area | Possible Celebrations |
| --- | --- |
| **Language arts** | **Publishing party.** Students share their published pieces with families, other classes, or younger students. |
| | **Genre/author celebration.** At the end of, say, a fairy tale unit, students dress as their favorite character, perform Readers Theater versions of fairy tales they've read, or do related art or science projects, such as building small houses of straw, wood, and Legos® for the story of *The Three Little Pigs*. |
| | **Poetry or word party.** Students have special time for reading poetry or finding interesting words. |
| **Math** | **Game day (or hour).** Children play games (especially board games) that get them practicing math skills in a fun and meaningful way. |
| | **End-of-unit party.** Students make quilts for geometry, for example, and picture books or posters to explain an operation such as multiplication. They then share these projects with classmates, other classes, or families. |
| **Social studies and science** | **Museum day.** Children show off research results, science experiments, or other special projects at the end of a unit. |
| | **Science party.** Students celebrate science by experiencing a variety of experiments or tools. For instance, at one station, they look through microscopes at different slides. At another, they combine certain materials (baking soda and vinegar!). At still another, they examine rocks with a hand lens and write about or sketch what they see. |

## Tips for Successful Celebrations

■ Keep it simple. Second graders enjoy festivities but may be easily overwhelmed and overstimulated. Plan for simple events where the focus is on learning and students' choices are few. For instance, students can perform a Readers Theater version of a book *or* do an art project related to the book, but they don't need to do both.

■ Prepare students. As with any change in routine, second graders will need a few days' advance notice of the special event, some sense of what will take place, and a chance to practice the tricky parts, such as how to talk to visitors who come up to their display on a museum day.

■ Be clear about your goals. Although celebrations are fun and create special memories for students, be careful not to have them "just because." Instead, think through how the celebration will help students learn, develop a love for school and learning, or offer a way to share their learning with their parents, and keep those goals in mind as you plan the event.

■ Use parent volunteers wisely. Parents can be helpful in planning and carrying out celebrations, but be sure you have a clear vision of what you want parents to do and give them specific guidance (whether to have decorations and how elaborate; how much food, if any, to bring; what kind of activities and how involved). For more on inviting families into the classroom, see Chapter 5, "Communicating with Parents."

## What About Holidays?

Although it can be fun for some children to celebrate Halloween and various winter holidays, celebrations may create uncomfortable situations for children and families who do not observe those holidays. Also, traditional school celebrations at these times of year often have no connection to the curriculum. So, if you can, put your party planning skills to use in other areas.

However, if your school requires such celebrations, here are some ideas for making them comfortable for everyone and giving them more purpose:

- Halloween. Have students dress up like favorite book characters and throw a party focused on literature. Or do activities around "scary stories." For instance, students could write and share their own scary stories, or after several days of reading many scary stories, students could rate them on their "scariness" or make "Wanted" posters for characters in some of them.

- Winter holidays. Include a variety of cultures in your winter holiday party. For example, have students share some food, games, or other tradition from their family's celebration of a holiday, whether a winter holiday or one from another season. (Be careful, though, to check your school or district's policy on bringing homemade foods into the classroom.) You could share folktales about a variety of the world's winter holidays.

- Valentine's Day. Celebrate friendships in the class by having students bring in valentines, write letters, or make cards for each other. Of course, you'll need to teach and model these skills first. Provide a list of names for everyone in the class and make sure students understand that they need to have cards for every person on the list. Or do a meaningful service project as a class, such as going to sing songs at a local nursing home or making valentines for service members overseas.

# Recess

Children who laugh and play together feel more connected to each other, so recess can be a great way to build community. Additionally, recess allows second graders to use and hone their rapidly developing gross motor skills. And it gives children a needed break from academics so they come back to the classroom recharged for their afternoon's work.

But these great benefits of recess will not come about automatically for all children. If we don't plan, teach, and guide students in practicing recess, some children will be unsure what to do, will hesitate to initiate or join play because they don't know how, or will play in a way that isn't safe for everyone. Even if you don't have recess duty, giving some attention to recess, especially during the first few weeks of school, will benefit students for the whole year. Here are some ideas to help recess run more smoothly.

## *Advocate for Different Types of Play*

Depending upon the constraints of your physical space, advocate, if you can, for students to have several recess options. Many schools have structures such as swings or monkey bars. Jump ropes, sidewalk chalk, and bubbles are welcome outdoor items. Some second graders also love structured play such as tag games or sports.

## *Teach Recess Behaviors*

It's best to teach recess behaviors on the playground by going out to recess with your class for the first few weeks of school. An occasional quick outdoor break during a nonrecess part of the day, if possible, gives extra practice opportunities while relaxing and refreshing the children (and you!). But you can teach a good deal of recess behavior inside, too.

To begin with, make sure students understand playground rules (these should be consistent with classroom rules and include, especially, safety and taking care of classmates). Use Interactive Modeling to teach essential recess behaviors and skills.

Things to model:

- Choosing what to do

- Using structures (swings, slides, etc.)

- Taking out and putting away equipment

- Getting an adult's attention

- Helping someone who's hurt

- Using the bathroom

- Staying within play area boundaries

- Responding to the lining-up signal

- Coming back into the building

- Asking a friend to play with you

- Joining a game already in progress

### Keeping Tag Games Safe for Everyone

Model and give your students time to practice several key skills to make sure tag games are safe for all:

- **Where and how to tag.** A good rule of thumb is to tag only on the back between the shoulders and hips. A tag should feel firm but gentle.

- **Avoiding collisions.** Model how to watch out for others and keep a safe distance (arm's length) from them as you move about and try to avoid getting tagged.

- **Tagger's choice.** Make sure students understand that if the person tagging believes he or she has tagged someone else, that person has to freeze even if she or he disagrees.

Stop the games at the earliest sign that students are getting rough and repractice these key skills. If just one student has trouble with any of these skills, have that student take a break from the game. At a later point, review and practice the expectations with that student.

## Introduce Recess Choices

To make informed choices about what they want to do at recess, children need to experience the possibilities beforehand. Spend the first week or two of school exploring all the recess options—what they look, feel, and sound like and what rules apply to them. You could, for example, spend a few days where everyone plays on the playground structures, a few days on tag and sports games (see the box on page 65 for ways to keep tag safe), and some time on choices like jumping rope and drawing with sidewalk chalk.

Even after you've introduced all the choices, occasionally plan days when you revisit some of them as a class so that students don't become stuck doing the same thing over and over.

## Observe and Support

If it's sometimes hard for us adults to start conversations with people we don't know or to invite a new acquaintance to go out socially, think how much harder similar socializing is for self-doubting second graders. Many of them become anxious when faced with a playground full of classmates who all look like they're happily engaged in fun activities. Even children who were quite adept just the year before at initiating or asking to join games may struggle a bit in second grade. So be sure to help. Even after you've taught these skills, spend time, if you can, watching students at recess to see if anyone is struggling and in need of extra support.

## Play With Students

If you have the opportunity, regularly supervising recess allows you to help resolve playground conflicts, and it gives you a great opportunity to observe students. Better yet, playing *with* the children lets you model good-natured play—how to laugh off getting tagged and how to be a good sport when tagging someone else, for example. You don't have to be an athlete to play. The point is to demonstrate friendly and safe playing.

Whole-group recess games such as tag and kickball definitely need adult oversight. Developmentally, second graders are not ready to manage such games on their own. Lead such games yourself, plan for another teacher or recess aide to organize and lead them, or have students make other choices on days when no adult leader can be present.

## Debrief

One strength of second graders is their ability to think deeply and reflect on experiences. You can let students exercise this strength while making recess more positive by taking a few minutes each day to reflect with the class about what's going well and why. Try to build on those positives and come back to them in future debriefing sessions.

# Lunchtime

Like recess, lunchtime can foster and deepen the sense of community in the class, but that is not likely to happen without some thought, planning, and teaching on your part. Without teacher intervention, lunch can be an isolating and painful time for some children. Here are some things you can do to help make lunchtime pleasant for all the children.

## Teach Lunchtime Behaviors

I was recently working with a school where some teachers were unhappy with their students' lunchtime behavior. After we listed the problems (not staying in their seats, taking too long in the line, etc.), I asked the teachers how they'd already tried to convey their lunchtime expectations to the

children. This query was met with a telling silence. The teachers realized they'd pretty much assumed that their students knew what to do at lunch and how to do it.

Even though second graders have been going to the cafeteria for a year or two, this is a new year, with new developmental challenges, a different teacher, possibly different expectations, and different classmates. At the start of each year, students need you to explain lunchtime rules clearly (ideally these are consistent with classroom rules), use Interactive Modeling to teach specific lunchroom behaviors, and give them plenty of practice. Behaviors and skills to teach:

■ Lining up for food

■ Paying or using a ticket system

■ Responding to the signal for attention

■ Staying in your seat

■ Talking with your tablemates

■ When and how to use the bathroom

■ Throwing away trash

■ Lining up for dismissal

■ Handling spills and cleaning tables and floors

## Assign Seats

Just as in the classroom, second graders may struggle with the stress of choosing seats in the lunchroom. You can assign seats quickly by announcing table groups for the week or placing post-its on the backs of chairs or on benches to indicate where students are to sit. Later in the year, if your class seems ready, try free seating sometimes (be sure to teach and model how to choose a seat and show friendliness to whoever sits down next to you).

## Teach Conversation Skills

Having assigned seats makes lunchtime easier for second graders, but it doesn't guarantee that they'll know how to talk to their neighbors once they get to their seats. Spend some classroom or lunchroom time practicing conversational skills by:

■ **Brainstorming topics.** With students, create a list of possible conversation topics: siblings, pets, sports, music, what they do after school, games they enjoy.

■ **Modeling conversations around those topics.** Choose a few topics and model how to talk about them.

■ **Having students practice and giving them feedback.** Have students partner off and practice their conversational skills. Notice what they're doing well and give them feedback.

■ **Debriefing after lunch.** Take a few minutes after lunch to let students share how their conversations went or what they learned about their classmates. Doing so regularly communicates your ongoing expectation that everyone will have someone to talk to at lunch.

## Eat With Students

Even if you're not required to eat with your students, try to do so as often as you can. At one school where I taught, teachers were required to eat lunch with their classes. Once I got over eating lunch at 10:40 a.m., I realized what a gift this obligation was to the children and to me: I learned so much about them during this relaxed, informal time.

Joining students at lunchtime will also give you a sense of what their lunch strengths are so you can build on those, what some of their struggles are, and who's having friendship issues.

### Plan a Calm and Quiet Ending to Lunch

Managed well, lunchtime is exciting and energizing for second graders. But they also benefit from some quiet for the last few minutes of lunchtime. They'll be able to fully relax, get a few more bites in (second graders are not natural multitaskers and often do not eat while socializing), and prepare for their transition back to the classroom. If you're able to be in the lunchroom with your students, use a visual or auditory signal to get their attention, let them know that lunch is almost over, and remind them of your expectation for that period of time (mainly eating and if they must talk, doing so with whispering voices, for instance).

# Closing Thoughts

When students feel that they belong, believe they're significant to people in their class, and have fun together, they develop bonds that keep them secure, motivated, and able to take the risks necessary to learn. We teachers can help students forge those bonds by giving them the chance to greet and share with each other throughout the year, carefully structuring recess and lunch, and planning meaningful and doable classroom celebrations. The resulting relaxed, happy, and enthusiastic feeling in your classroom will make your efforts worthwhile.

## CHAPTER 4

# Classroom Games, Special Projects, and Field Trips

**A**ll children need school to be a happy, lively, and engaging place, and second graders are no different. Games, songs, special projects, and field trips can add much-needed liveliness and joy to second graders' school days. Some of my second graders' best learning and fondest memories come from singing together, acting out ancient Egyptian mythology, and caring for caterpillars to release as butterflies in the spring.

These kinds of learning are important because they do so much to help children take in and remember content, while also creating both in-the-moment and long-lasting excitement for learning itself. Other kinds of learning—such as reading, writing, or doing math problems—are certainly valuable and necessary. But games, songs, special projects, and field trips serve a unique and vital role.

Games are fun, build community, and help students see and learn content in new and different ways from pencil-and-paper tasks. Singing together builds a sense of community, energizes students, and gives them a chance to be playful. It can also help second graders develop important literacy skills. Special projects and field trips can bring a unit's or lesson's goals to life and help children apply what they have learned in meaningful contexts—ultimately leading to more lasting learning. For example, when children use fractional measurements to make their own class recipe for trail mix, most will remember what they learned about fractions longer than they'll remember the most well-thought-out and executed direct instruction.

In this chapter, you'll find tips for making your curriculum and school day come alive by working games, activities, and special projects into your schedule as often as possible.

73

## Finding Time for Lively Learning

In my experience, the best way to find time for engaging, playful activities is to gently weave academics into the special things we already do with children. For instance, when playing Simon Says, work in some academic review: "Simon says to raise your hand and tell me one spelling rule we've learned this year." You could also play a categories game in which children take turns offering words that fit a certain spelling pattern, equations to match a target number, or facts they discovered in their research. The key is to keep the academics light and the focus on fun.

# Classroom Games

Playing games, singing songs, and reciting chants and poems together are great ways for students to build community while learning and practicing new information and skills. Second graders enjoy a wide variety of games, songs, chants, and poems, but as with all things second grade, they need structure and support, even in a playful context. Following are some considerations to keep in mind.

## *Avoid Competitive Games With Winners and Losers*

Although there is a place for healthy competition in children's lives, one key reason for playing whole-group games in the classroom is to build students' sense of belonging to their community, so choose games that will foster that feeling. Adapt competitive or elimination games to make them more inclusive. For example:

■ **Freeze Dance.** In Freeze Dance, children traditionally dance to music and freeze when the music stops. Those who don't freeze have to leave the game for a while. In a new version called Opposite World Freeze Dance that my colleague Susan Roser teaches, students who move when the music stops continue playing, but in the opposite way—freezing when the music starts and dancing when the music stops. (Roser's book *Energizers!*—see the box "Learn More About Indoor Games" on page 75— explains this and many other inclusive games.)

■ Hot Potato. The traditional game Hot Potato has children passing an object around until the caller, whose back is to the group, announces "Hot potato!" The child holding the object at that moment is out. You can play this game more inclusively by creating an inner and outer hot potato circle. Students in each circle pass objects. When the caller says "Hot potato," the two students "caught" holding the objects quickly change spots, and play continues.

**Learn More About Indoor Games**

*99 Activities and Greetings: Great for Morning Meeting . . . and Other Meetings, Too!* by Melissa Correa-Connolly (Center for Responsive Schools, 2004).

*Energizers! 88 Quick Movement Activities That Refresh and Refocus* by Susan Lattanzi Roser (Center for Responsive Schools, 2009).

Note, though, that games with winners and losers may be appropriate for pairs of students when an element of luck is involved, such as the roll of a die or turning over cards placed in random order. Children can take winning or losing less personally in these cases. Even so, you may still want to talk with students about the role of luck or chance. Or you can add an element of surprise as to who wins by having students spin a spinner at the end of the game, for instance, to determine whether having more cards or fewer cards makes someone the winner.

## Have the Class Try to Beat Its Own Record

One way to retain the excitement of competition without having winners and losers is to have the class compete as a team. The class could try to reach a common goal, surpass its own highest score, or beat the clock. For example, the class could see how many homophones they can come up with as a team in five minutes.

## Provide Clear Directions

Even when playing light-hearted, fun games, second graders can become anxious if they're unsure what to do. Explain the directions clearly, and then play a practice round to show how the game goes. Make clear that this practice round is just to learn the game and that you expect mistakes and will explain anything students don't understand.

### Great Classroom Games for Second Graders

■ **Squeeze Number.** Hang a number line low enough for the children to reach. Give two children, or "squeezers," a small piece of paper each to cover a number and thus mark out a range of numbers. For instance, one child might cover 4 and the other 52. You think of a number between 4 and 52—say, 29. As the class tries to guess the number, you tell them if their guess is too high or too low, and the squeezers move accordingly. If a child guessed 25, you'd say "too low," and the squeezer covering 4 would move to 25. Continue taking guesses until the class guesses your number.

■ **Would You Rather?** Ask students a "Would you rather" question that has four answers: "Would you rather visit an Egyptian pyramid, go on a real archaeological dig, unwrap a mummy, or sail down the Nile?" Designate one corner of the room for each answer. Students walk quietly and safely to the corner for their chosen answer. They return to the circle, you ask another question, and so on.

■ **Zoom.** Children begin by simply passing the word "zoom" smoothly around the circle. For more challenge, you can time students to see how long it takes them to "zoom" around. Eventually, you can give a few children another word to say, such as "eek," which reverses the direction of the "zoom."

## Choose Games Everyone Can Play Confidently

Second graders tend to be self-conscious, so avoid or change games that might make them anxious. Take a game like "Sparkle," in which students go around the circle to spell words aloud, each student adding one letter. Second graders may not be good enough spellers to hold all the prior letters in their heads while also anticipating the next letter. If you have any doubts about a game, skip it and choose one that you're sure all students can play successfully.

## Plan Some Partner Games

Second graders work especially well with partners, so it's a great year to use partner games in various curricular areas. For instance:

■ **Card flip.** Each child takes half a deck of cards. The children each flip over two cards from their decks and add them together to see who has the highest sum.

■ **Spelling board game.** Make a simple board game in which the spots on the board require players to spell certain words or give examples of words that fit certain spelling patterns. Children pair up to play the game.

To help partner games go smoothly:

- **Pair up children with similar academic skills.** Problems can result if a highly skilled speller gets bored waiting for his or her partner to figure out how to spell a word or if a child who's struggling with certain skills is intimidated by a partner to whom everything seems to come easily.

- **Model and practice sportsmanship.** When you introduce games, model how to decide quickly and without arguing who goes first. Also teach students skills like laughing it off when things don't go your way and encouraging your partner when his or her luck takes a turn for the worse.

## Sprinkle Songs, Chants, Energizers, and Poems Throughout the Day

Singing or chanting together, moving around in a quick activity, or reciting poems together—these are all good ways to help second graders keep their moods light and feel the sense of belonging that's so important to success at school. The variety of songs, chants, energizers, and poems second graders enjoy is virtually endless. Tips to help you choose and use these successfully:

- **Sing, even if you're not a "good" singer!** So often teachers say they don't "do singing" with their students because they can't sing well. I'm not the best singer in the world either, but students never seem to mind. In fact, I think my own willingness to belt out songs despite my limits as a singer encourages students to take their own risks and join in. If you really feel you cannot sing, use a CD, rather than depriving your students of the joy of singing.

- **Scaffold for success.** Begin the year with short, catchy tunes, easy-to-follow movement games, and songs that children can learn quickly and then vary. For instance, in the song, "Peanut Butter, Grape Jelly," children are challenged in each round to replace "grape jelly" with another food to go with peanut butter. I've seen students have so much fun with this ("peanut butter, tuna!"). Later in the year, you can add more complex songs or do songs in rounds.

**Learn More About Songs and Chants**

*Energizers! 88 Quick Movement Activities That Refresh and Refocus* by Susan Lattanzi Roser (Center for Responsive Schools, 2009).

■ **Show song lyrics or words to poems.** Put them on charts or project them onto a screen. Many students need the support of the written text to feel confident with singing or reciting, and this written text can also help many develop their literacy skills.

■ **Avoid songs or chants second graders may consider "babyish."** Second graders often like to distance themselves from their first grade selves by looking down on things they may have enjoyed just a few months before. Choose songs that are new to them. Or put a new spin on old favorites—for instance, work with the children to write your own version of an old favorite like "The Itsy Bitsy Spider."

■ **Be willing to join in and be silly yourself.** Although second graders can be very silly, on many days they will almost need permission to relax and cut loose. By singing with gusto and doing all the silly accompanying movements, you can give second graders the go-ahead to ease up, enjoy their playful sides, and get the most out of these singing and movement breaks.

# Special Projects

With their improving gross and fine motor abilities and attention to detail, second graders benefit tremendously from special art, science, or social studies projects. In the second grade classes I've taught, children have loved making a wide variety of books. During our annual insect study, they've enjoyed making papier-mâché versions of the insects they were researching. The following guidelines will help you keep your special projects manageable and fun.

## Plan Bite-Sized Projects

Second graders like to finish things; they value their end products. So plan projects they can complete relatively quickly, either independently or with minimal adult assistance. I've had students make mini-books (second

graders like little things) that are based on books we've read aloud. For instance, after reading *Some Things Are Scary* by Florence Parry Heide, students wrote about and illustrated on each page something that scared them. Most students completed seven to ten pages in a few days, and then we gave the books an interesting cover (cardstock works, as does covering thin cardboard with decorative paper or a digital photo).

## Be Sure of Your Learning and Curricular Goals

Sure, it would be fun for the class to make bread, but if you cannot clarify to yourself and the students exactly what they're to learn from the project, it may not be the best use of school time. Share your learning goals for projects with students. For example, for a poster-making project during a unit on the Pilgrims and Wampanoag natives, you might say "Today we are going to make posters to show what we have learned about different parts of the Wampanoags' lives. This project will help us reflect on our learning, learn how to organize information effectively, and give everyone a chance to learn about the things they did not study."

## Be Careful With Examples of Finished Products

Being somewhat risk-averse, second graders often copy the models you show them. One year, my class made a quilt. They were each to choose a line that resonated with meaning for them from one of Patricia Polacco's books, write that line as the border for their quilt square, and then illustrate it in the center. I made a square as an example and was disappointed to discover that so many children's initial drafts looked very similar to my own! We went back to the drawing board, but this added time to the project for which I hadn't planned.

I learned over time to brainstorm ideas first before showing students models, to use several models, or, if possible, to save projects from prior years to give students even more ideas.

## *Give Students Choices When Possible*

All of us do best and are most motivated when we have choices. Because second graders pride themselves on their individuality, they especially benefit from having a choice about what to study, what to do for a project, or what materials to use. Having choices also gives second graders important practice in risk-taking. If, for example, the class is doing topic studies on insects or animals, students can choose which creature to study and whether they'd like to present their learning by making a poster or writing a summary of the most important things they discovered.

See the section "Class Celebrations" on page 61 in Chapter 3 for ideas of projects to celebrate the end of a unit, an author the class especially enjoys, or a whole curricular area.

# Field Trips

Visits to art galleries, nature centers, nearby plant or animal habitats, the local bakery, dairy, or grocery store . . . field trips can provide unique and interesting learning experiences that make second grade content come alive. For one social studies unit, our class read many well-written and beautifully illustrated books about how certain things were produced (*Ice Cream* by Elisha Cooper was one of our favorites). But a trip to our local bread company provided a real-world illustration of the concepts we were studying. The children delighted in seeing the huge mixers and processing machines, stepping on the delivery truck, and watching the on-site store in action.

Nonetheless, second graders look upon field trips with mixed emotions. They're often thrilled and excited about the prospect of discovery, but at the same time they may be quite anxious about leaving the comfort of their school day and schedule. As with most things second grade, some careful thought and planning can help you build on students' enthusiasm without letting their nerves get the best of them. Your school's traditions and your units of study will guide your choice of field trips. But no matter where you go, the following tips will help you get there and back smoothly and safely, both emotionally and physically.

**Addressing the "What If" Questions**

For my first field trip with second graders, I was completely unprepared for the onslaught of "What if" questions that popped up: "What if we get lost?" "What if we don't get back in time for lunch?" "What if we can't find the bathrooms?" As I let child after child ask these questions, it seemed as if the children were spreading nervousness to each other and scaring themselves. Here are a few solutions for helping students stay calm before a field trip:

■ **Anticipate worries.** Be sure to cover them all during your planning sessions with the class.

■ **Field "What if" questions privately.** Let students know that you would be happy to answer "What if" questions in private. Give them a place to record questions that occur to them.

■ **Enlist parents' help.** Give parents a heads-up about this "What if" phenomenon so they can help allay their children's anxieties.

## Give Children the Facts Beforehand

81

As with any break from their routine, second graders need to know in advance what to expect on a field trip. A week or two is usually fine unless you need a great deal of parent help with the trip. Things to tell them:

■ **The five Ws and one H.** Where they'll be going and why, when they'll be going, how they'll get there, who they'll meet there, and what they'll do and see there (include some examples).

■ **Bathroom information.** Where the bathrooms will be—especially important information for second graders.

■ **How missed work will be handled.** Changes in routine cause anxiety in second graders, so let them know what parts of school they'll miss and how they'll "make up" what they missed.

## Use Familiar Routines and Procedures

Second graders will be comforted if they're able to follow as many of their regular routines and procedures on field trips as possible. Use the same signals you use in the classroom to gain attention on the field trip. Employ the same procedures for transitions and lining up. Just as you assign seats and partners in the classroom, assign partners for the bus ride or tasks on the trip.

## Practice What You Can

Practicing some of the especially challenging parts of the trip will help second graders relax and enjoy themselves. For instance:

■ **Practice getting there.** Set up chairs in the room like bus seats and practice being on the bus together and following bus rules.

■ **Practice being there.** Depending on where you're going, you can also practice what to do when you get there. When our class was going to two grocery stores to compare prices and other factors as part of a social studies unit, we practiced with an in-class grocery store.

Keep the practice light, fun, and fast-paced.

## Think About Bathroom Needs

Second graders worry a lot about when and whether they will be able to use the bathroom. Make sure to leave some bathroom time before you go, and have a plan for where and how students will go once you arrive. Check the bathroom situation with your host and think about whether you'll be comfortable having other adults take students to those facilities or whether you'll need to do so yourself.

## Think About Lunch Needs

It's best for second graders, with their love of routine, if you try to arrange field trips so that they don't clash with your regularly scheduled lunchtime. When that's not possible, a little planning will make lunch "on the road" a little easier:

■ **Collect everyone's lunches before you leave.** Second graders often have an understandably hard time keeping up with their lunches while on a field trip, so put all the lunches in a cardboard box or two and make sure every student has a lunch. (If the cafeteria is providing lunches, they'll often pack them in cardboard boxes.)

■ **Plan where students will eat.** Check with the location where you'll be having the field trip to see if they have enough space for the children to eat at tables. If not, see if you can round up some cloth or paper tablecloths or blankets to take so that students won't have to eat on the ground.

■ **Pack hand sanitizer.** Make sure students use it before eating. You may also want to pack a few napkins, paper towels, or wipes to help students with spills or food on their hands and faces.

## Give Students Concrete Tasks to Help Their Learning

Second graders are doers. They'll do best on field trips when given developmentally appropriate tasks to accomplish. Some tools that give structure and purpose:

■ Scavenger hunts

■ Recording sheets for key observations

■ Checklists of what to see or do

## Reflect on Field Trip Learning

Finally, make the most of field trips by leading students to reflect or follow up in some way on what they learned. You might have students make a "top ten" list of what they learned, write a thank-you letter with specific details to the people at the site, or write captions for photographs you took while on the trip.

# Closing Thoughts

By engaging their minds in exciting ways, classroom games, songs, special projects, and field trips bring a sense of playfulness to school, help children learn more deeply, and help them better remember what they learn. Just as important, these ways of learning help second graders build the sense of safety and community that encourages them to take the risks so important to learning. Carefully interspersing opportunities for lively, playful learning throughout the school day and year will ensure that children are more positive about school, more excited about learning, and more likely to retain what they learn.

## CHAPTER 5

# Communicating
# With Parents

Open and empathetic communication with parents helps the school year go more smoothly, no matter what grade you teach. In second grade, parents need information not only about how you'll be guiding their child's learning, but also about the typical but sometimes baffling developmental changes their child is going through. Communicating this information early and often helps alleviate any concerns parents may have, encourages them to support their child's learning, and helps them recognize and enjoy the uniquely wonderful aspects of second graders.

Like teachers, parents often work in isolation, and they often can use a little help from us to put things in perspective. I recall one parent's frustrated call to me about how she and her daughter were having regular homework battles. I was so taken aback, as this was a child who happily did every school assignment and most of the time went above and beyond the requirements.

After digging a little deeper, I learned that the parent wanted the homework done as soon as school was over. I gently suggested the child might need a little break from school-type work in the afternoon, and we decided the parent should ask the child to choose from that time of day and two others. The child ultimately chose to have a snack and play

**About the Term "Parent"**

Students come from a variety of homes with a variety of family structures. Many children are being raised by grandparents, siblings, aunts and uncles, and foster families. All of these people are to be honored for devoting their time, attention, and love to raising children. Coming up with one word that encompasses all these caregivers is challenging. For simplicity's sake, this chapter uses the word "parent" to refer to anyone who is the child's primary caregiver.

outside and then return to do homework shortly before dinner. The problem was solved. Of course, it isn't always this simple to help parents, but having open lines of communication makes solutions more possible.

In this chapter, we'll look at key communication strategies and consider ways to respond to specific concerns of second grade parents.

# Strategies for Good Communication

These strategies will help you build a firm foundation for all of your communication with parents. Remember that communication goes both ways. In all of your contacts with parents—formal and informal—be sure to offer your own information but also to gather parents' insights about their children. Listen especially for information about the family that can help you better work with the student (for instance, the mother just had a baby, or both parents work the night shift while another family member stays with the child and prepares her for school in the morning).

## *Start Reaching Out Early—With Positives!*

Start communicating with parents early—before the school year starts, if you've received your class list. Extend a friendly welcome and briefly describe what students will be learning this year. Once school starts, communicate with parents as soon as possible about the strengths you're seeing in their child. When your first contact about a child is positive, the child sees that you're noticing her or his strengths, you build rapport with parents, and you help ease any anxiety parents may be feeling about their child's year. With this positive foundation, parents are also more likely to see you as an ally if a problem comes up for their child later in the year.

Some ways you can reach out:

■ **Introductory letter.** A friendly letter before or just as school begins is a good way to introduce yourself to parents, provide an overview of the year, and convey your excitement about teaching their child. Keep your letter brief, and remember to let parents know how and when they can contact you.

Dear Parents and Caregivers,

I'm very excited about teaching your child this year and want to let you know a little about myself and second grade. I'm from Nashville originally, enjoy spending time with my large family and my dog Mudge, and like to read, cook, and garden. This will be my 13th year as a teacher. I've taught other grades but have a special fondness for second graders.

Second grade is an exciting year. In second grade, children become stronger readers, math students, writers, and spellers. They can focus on their work for longer periods than in first grade and do more careful work.

Our second grade curriculum covers ancient Egypt; the Pilgrims and the Wampanoag natives; weighing, measuring, and economics; and butterflies and insects. We'll develop literacy skills and have daily spelling, reading, and writing workshops. We'll learn new math skills such as multidigit addition, multidigit subtraction, and simple multiplication, and we'll begin learning geometry concepts.

In the first days of school, I'll ask the children what they'd like to learn and accomplish this year. As a class, we'll then create classroom rules that will enable all class members to fulfill their school hopes and dreams.

When we meet at Parent Night, I'd love to hear your thoughts. What are one or two academic and social goals for your child that we can work on together? I'll also share my hopes and dreams for the year, and I'll be happy to answer any questions you might have.

If you'd like to be in touch before then, please call (xxx-xxx-xxx) any day before 9 PM or email me (ms_wilson@school.org) anytime. I look forward to meeting you and hope you continue to enjoy your summer.

■ **Informal classroom visits.** Set up a time in late summer when parents and children can stop by school, meet you, and see the second grade classroom. Keep your conversations brief and positive.

■ **Phone calls and email.** A quick call or email home to report on a child's progress early in the year lets parent know you're focused on the positives: "David has written several funny pieces about life with his baby brother. He is definitely finding his voice as a writer. He is also very cooperative and goes out of his way to help teachers and friends."

### Emailing Parents

In general, serious or confidential matters are best discussed in person, by phone, or in a paper-and-envelope letter. But email can be great for quick notes about day-to-day classroom life. A few things to consider:

■ **Know if parents can—and want to—use email.** At the fall open house, invite parents to sign up to receive email from you if they'd like. Tell them you'll also be communicating in other ways. Judge by the number of sign-ups whether to use email regularly.

■ **Keep the volume of messages manageable by mixing in other ways of communicating.** Most parents rely less on email once they know you'll be sharing news in various ways.

■ **Follow the guidelines.** Check whether your school, district, or parent organization has guidelines for emailing families.

■ **Formal open house ("Parent Night").** These early fall gatherings offer a good in-person opportunity to connect with parents. You can talk about exciting things happening in the classroom, display some of the children's work, and share ways parents can support their children during the school year. It's also a good time to share a little written information about common characteristics of second graders. (See "Share Information about Child Development" on page 90.) Avoid getting into conversations with parents about their individual child—schedule another time to talk with any parents who raise concerns that apply only to their child.

■ **Website.** If your school has a website with a page for each teacher and you know that most of your parents have Internet access, that page can be a good place to post general information about classroom happenings and children's development in second grade. (Be sure to find out your school's or district's guidelines for class websites or webpages.)

## Listen

Parents are experts on their own children and can give you valuable insights that will help you teach their child. Whenever you communicate with parents, make it a two-way street by inviting them to share their thoughts and insights.

## Empathize

Parents want to help their children succeed, and they feel pain when their child struggles. For some parents, any communication from the teacher triggers nervousness and worry. For others, negative school experiences of their own—or other personal or family issues—make dealing with school issues difficult

> **Do Parents Have Language or Literacy Issues?**
>
> Be alert for indications that students' parents have difficulty reading. If so, be careful about relying on written information too often. Look for other ways to communicate, such as phone calls or recorded messages that parents can call in to receive.

for them. Any parent, when concerned about their child, may state their cares in ways that seem offensive or critical to us. My very wise first principal coached me to avoid lashing back, as nothing positive results from that. Hearing parents out without interrupting or getting defensive pays off in the long run. Try to put yourself in parents' shoes. Remind yourself that their harsh words are not about you, but about their concerns for their child.

## Communicate Regularly and Consistently

Once you're into the swing of the school year, regularly send home information about what's going on in the classroom. Keep the information brief, focused, and positive. Good topics are classroom activities and accomplishments, upcoming events, and common developmental changes children go through in second grade. Also be sure to address any concerns that a number of parents have recently raised. For example, if several parents

have recently raised reading issues with you, you might share some information about reading development with a note like the following:

**Reading**

Several of you have recently said you are worried whether your child is reading books of the right level. Developmentally, it is very common for second graders to read books that seem easy. Their brains are actually doing the important step of organizing and solidifying their reading skills. Reading short and simple books helps them do this. Once children complete this phase, they will naturally begin to move toward harder books and to read more for pleasure on their own. Be patient—they will get there.

In the meantime, you can support them at home by being positive about their reading, making all reading experiences as fun and pleasant as possible, and reading aloud to them as often as you can.

Keep letting me know about your concerns. It helps our whole class.

Whether you send home a letter or newsletter, use email, or post updates on a webpage, set a routine and stick to it. A consistent schedule and format increases the chances that parents will read and respond to whatever information you provide.

## Share Information About Child Development

It can be confusing or worrisome for parents to see their children go through developmental changes, even if these changes are common. Sharing child development information reassures parents and encourages them to look for growth in their own child, rather than comparing the child with friends or classmates. It also helps parents see you as a knowledgeable partner who understands their child's needs.

I've found it helpful to give parents written information about characteristics common in their child's grade, like the Yardsticks Guide Series based on Chip Wood's book *Yardsticks: Child and Adolescent Development Ages 4–14*

**Child Development Resources for Parents**

*Yardsticks: Child and Adolescent Development Ages 4–14* by Chip Wood (Center for Responsive Schools, 2017).

Yardsticks Guide Series: Common Developmental Characteristics in the Classroom and at Home (Center for Responsive Schools, 2018; based on *Yardsticks* by Chip Wood).

(Center for Responsive Schools, 2017). They can then refer to this information throughout the year.

Key points to make as you talk with families about their second grader's development:

■ **Children develop at different rates.** Human growth and development is complex, and no two children will reach the same developmental stage at exactly the same time. Second graders, for example, are commonly ready to do more complex mental mathematics, but some will show this readiness early in the year and some later.

■ **Different aspects of development occur at different rates.** For example, one child might pick up math skills very quickly but need more time to learn friendship skills. Another may make friends easily but need more time to get the hang of second grade reading.

■ **Children will change as the year progresses.** In second grade, for example, a child may prefer to work alone or with one other child at the beginning of the year (common among second graders) but increasingly enjoy group work toward the middle or end of the year (common among third graders).

■ **Growth often happens in fits and starts.** Children may go through an explosive period of growth followed by a lag or even a regression.

- Second graders often show tremendous growth in thinking, attention, and communication. Many are also developing good listening skills and excellent recall. The result is that many second graders become "experts" on various topics and begin to show strengths in particular subjects.

- Second graders can be moody and inward. This is common. Adults can help by showing empathy and modeling healthy, appropriate reactions to life's ups and downs.

### Let Parents Know How They Can Help

Try to survey parents early in the year—do they speak a different language, have strong clerical skills, or possess artistic talents? Besides sharing specific skills, most parents can also walk with small groups of children on field trips or help with science, social studies, or art projects. Letting parents know that you'll be welcoming them into the classroom helps them feel like partners in their child's education. (For more on having parents in the classroom, see "Involving Parents in Events and Activities" on page 98.)

# Special Concerns of Second Grade Parents

Although each child is unique, second graders do often share a common set of behaviors and academic issues that may worry their parents. Here are some of parents' more common concerns, along with helpful ways to respond.

### Friendship Issues

Some second graders are aloof and choosy, preferring to play with one other friend—although that one other friend may change frequently. One year before, however, they were probably quite social and liked to interact with a variety of classmates, which is common in first graders. Parents seeing this change may worry that their child has regressed socially.

Reassure parents that changing friends or wanting just one friend at a time is common in children in second grade. Parents can support their child in expanding and maintaining friendships by:

■ **Listening without comment.** Parents can listen without too much comment or judgment to their child's tales about friendship. ("So you're enjoying playing with Ethan now? What have you guys been doing?" instead of "Why aren't you playing with Andreas anymore? Did you guys have a fight?")

■ **Giving extra encouragement.** Parents can also gently encourage their child to accept invitations to play dates with a variety of friends.

■ **Avoiding comparisons.** Parents should avoid comparing their own childhood friendships with those of their child. Second graders are understandably likely to interpret comments such as "When I was your age, I had a best friend" or "When I was your age, I played with lots of people and didn't have any trouble inviting them to play" as criticism rather than encouragement.

## Emotional Sensitivity

Some second graders become more introverted and moodier than they were as first graders, perhaps even seeming worried or preoccupied. You can help parents understand that this is a common phase. In the meantime, encourage parents to:

■ **Listen without giving too much advice.** Parents should listen with full attention to their child's worries or complaints but refrain from offering a lot of problem-solving. Paraphrasing and empathizing work better:

"So you worked all morning on that drawing, but it didn't come out the way you wanted. Boy, that must be frustrating."

■ **Avoid "catastrophizing" their child's issues.** Treating every problem like a crisis heightens children's anxiety and lessens their coping skills, whereas a matter-of-fact reaction calms and reassures.

■ **Help their child relax.** Providing quiet time and space can help when their child seems anxious or upset.

**Is There Something to Parents' Worries?**

At the same time that you're reassuring parents about their child's friendships or moods, observe the child (during recess, if necessary) to make sure there isn't a serious problem. If you see any worrisome signs, talk to your school or district guidance counselor, psychologist, or social worker for advice on next steps.

## Academic Progress

Second graders frequently dislike taking risks. When given a choice, they often select easier assignments, which may leave parents feeling that their child is not challenged or is not gaining ground academically.

Explain to parents that during second grade, children are often consolidating skills they began developing when they were first graders. As a result, their growth may look less dramatic than it did in first grade. Children may, for example, need to read books at the same level for a while to solidify their reading skills and to build their tolerance for taking risks. If parents understand this aspect of development, many "problems" will seem less troublesome.

To support their child's growth toward taking risks and enjoying challenges, parents can:

■ **Provide support and feedback.** Encourage parents to provide lots of specific feedback about what their child is doing well, rather than focusing on what the child is not doing well.

■ **Encourage small risks.** Share with parents the value of encouraging *small* risks and taking positive note, without overdoing it, when their child takes a risk, even if the end result is unsuccessful.

■ **Talk to you.** Invite parents to raise any concerns with you, not their child.

94

## Tiny Handwriting

Many parents are puzzled or annoyed by the tiny printing style their child may adopt during second grade. Assure parents that small printing is actually quite common in second graders and encourage them to focus on the content of their child's writing, rather than the size of the letters.

## Homework

Homework—long an issue for parents, teachers, and students—can be especially problematic for second graders, who tend to be perfectionistic and risk-averse. Some ways to make homework more successful for students and less worrying for their parents:

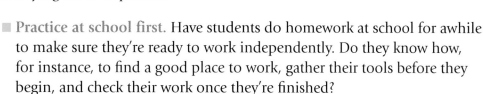

■ **Practice at school first.** Have students do homework at school for awhile to make sure they're ready to work independently. Do they know how, for instance, to find a good place to work, gather their tools before they begin, and check their work once they're finished?

■ **Avoid having second graders copy assignments from the board.** Second graders typically find this task very difficult. Better ideas: Give parents a written overview of the week's homework or have children place each night's homework in a homework folder.

■ **Choose tasks second graders can do on their own.** Parents can read directions and provide structure, but if homework requires teaching or coaching, conflict often results. So give assignments that second graders can do without help (for example, measuring things in their home, or finding words from newspapers and magazines that fit a certain pattern they've studied).

■ **Keep homework short.** Be conservative in estimating how long assignments will take. Think about the more deliberate and careful children in the class.

■ **Let students and parents know how to handle homework problems.** If you're comfortable with calls about homework, tell students and families when they can call you. Also let parents know it's OK to end a homework session that's becoming too stressful. Perfectionistic second graders will be more willing to take this option if you let them know they may occasionally feel stressed in this way, and if they do, stopping homework is an acceptable solution.

■ **Be sensitive to family difficulties.** Some children live in very cramped apartments. Some stay in a different homeless shelter each night. Many children in these and other difficult situations try hard to do their homework but can't find the necessary space, time, and quiet. You can help by modifying their assignments or finding time at school for them to do their homework.

## Productive Parent-Teacher Conferences

Parent-teacher conferences are great opportunities to deepen your relationship with parents and discuss any concerns about a child's academic or social progress. As in all your communications with parents, it's important at these conferences to listen, empathize, and be ready to share information. Following are additional techniques that will help parent-teacher conferences go smoothly.

## Offer Conversation Starters

To put parents at ease and get the conversation flowing, have some questions ready: "What did your child like about school last year?" "What does she like to do at home?" "What are your hopes for him this year?" Be ready to redirect the conversation if a parent should raise concerns or critiques of last year's teacher. You might say for instance, "Because our time is so limited, I'd like to focus on what we can do well this year" or "I hear your concerns about last year, but it would still help me to know what your child did enjoy so that we can build on those positives."

If appropriate for the parents of your students, you might want to send these questions home in written form at the start of the year, rather than asking in person. Then both you and the parents will have time to think about the questions and possible responses.

## Invite Parents to Share Their Thoughts

We teachers often have so much we want to convey at conferences that we forget to listen to what parents have to say. Give parents plenty of time to voice their concerns and ask questions. As experts on their child, they have valuable insights to share and will appreciate your respectful recognition of their role in helping their child. "Please tell me what you think" or "What have you been noticing?" are simple ways to signal that you want to hear what parents have to say.

## Highlight the Positives

When children are struggling, it's more important than ever for parents to recognize their skills and accomplishments. Discuss struggles fully and honestly, but also tell parents about their child's strengths and ways they can build on those strengths. For example, "Eric has a very well-developed sense of fairness for his age. He'll speak up when he thinks someone has wronged him or a friend. We're working on using a calm tone and finding the right time to voice his concerns. But not every child thinks so deeply about justice and takes action the way Eric does. It's a real strength."

## Address Just One or Two Concerns

If your list is exhaustive, parents (and their child) can feel defeated. You can mention that there are several things you'd like to work on with the child, but that for now you're going to concentrate on just one or two. Grouping issues under common themes helps limit the discussion. For example, "I've noticed that May rushes though her work and also blurts out answers without waiting her turn. Do you notice her being impulsive in similar ways at home?"

### *Let Parents Know If You Need Thinking Time*

Sometimes we can be more helpful if we refrain from rushing in with solutions or advice. It's OK to tell parents that you want to think through what they've said, observe their child in light of new information, consult others, or read up on an issue they've raised. "Wow, I didn't realize Stacy is struggling so much with homework. In class, she's always pretty focused. I'd like to talk with her more about this issue and think about how we can make homework a better experience for everyone." Be sure to follow up and let the parents know what you discovered and how you think you might address the issue.

## Involving Parents in Events and Activities

Whether playing games with their parents at a school math night, having their parents come on a field trip, or just sitting with their parents at lunch, second graders welcome their parents' involvement in school. Many parents also enjoy these special times with their child. Additionally, having parents help in class or at special events can enable you to do projects you couldn't do otherwise.

Following are some tips on structuring parent involvement to maximize the benefits for everyone.

### *Set Expectations for Parents*

Let parents know what they'll be doing and how many children they'll be working with, and make sure they know the classroom rules (second graders can become very confused if parents fail to follow classroom rules). Following are sample written guidelines you could send home, pass out when parents visit, or read aloud as children and adult visitors listen together.

# Sample Written Guidelines for Parent Volunteers

*Thanks for volunteering in our class.* It means a great deal to your child and our whole class that you're willing to share your time with us.

Here are some guidelines to help you when you volunteer:

- If you have any questions about what you should be doing in the classroom, feel free to ask me.

- When I ring my chime or raise my hand, it means the students should stop talking and look at me. It helps if we adults do the same.

- If you're helping students with a project, try to make sure children do as much of the work as possible, take turns, and help clean up. If you give out materials, have all students keep hands in their laps and wait until everyone has what they need.

- If you're working with a small group, please follow our class rules by speaking to the children respectfully and calmly.

- Most students love working with a parent volunteer, so things will probably go smoothly. But if you are concerned about a child's behavior, please let me know. Feel free to positively redirect children. ("Keep your hands to yourself," "Stay close to me," "Quiet voices.") But if any further disciplinary steps are needed, please let me handle them.

- If a student should have a problem, please protect that child's privacy by not discussing the issue with others.

## Maintain Consistent Discipline

It's important that you remain the teacher at all times when parents are present. Don't expect or allow parents to discipline other people's children. In fact, second graders, who are already risk-averse and reluctant to admit their mistakes, may feel unsafe when an adult they don't know well corrects their misbehavior.

Sometimes second graders cling to their visiting parents, have a harder time following the teacher's directions, or try to make their friends laugh through their interactions with their parents. Be ready to step in and respectfully let the child know that classroom rules apply even when their parent is present. The following chart shows some typical situations and ways you might respond.

## When Children Misbehave During Family Visits

| Situation | What You Might Say or Do |
|---|---|
| Samantha's mother is helping Samantha and her table group mix the ingredients for a recipe. Samantha keeps trying to crawl into her mother's lap. Samantha's mom has asked her several times to go back to her seat, but Samantha does not stay there. | "Samantha, your mom is here to help everyone at your table. Come sit with me so she can do that. You can try again in a few minutes." |
| Charlie ordinarily follows the rules and cooperates quickly and quietly. But when his dad chaperones him and a few classmates on a field trip to a nature center, Charlie keeps running ahead of his group. His father is trying to keep both Charlie and the rest of the group safe. | "Charlie, show me that you can stay with your dad's group." If Charlie persists: "Charlie, come join my group for awhile. You can rejoin your dad later." |
| Lucy's aunt comes for lunch, and they have a great time together, but when it's time for her aunt to leave, Lucy becomes very clingy and cries for her aunt not to go. Her aunt seems at a loss. | Gently take Lucy by the hand. "Lucy, I know it's hard to say good-bye to your aunt. Let's return to the classroom, and maybe you can make something for her or write to her at quiet time." Signal for the aunt to leave. |

## Give Parents Nonteaching Roles

Unless parents are also teachers, they likely won't have the skills needed to effectively coach or teach math, writing, or other academics. It's best, therefore, to invite parents to help with special projects or events while doing the day-to-day instruction yourself.

## Try to Involve All Parents in Some Way

Second graders often feel confused or hurt if their parents don't help out while others' parents do. You can help by looking for ways for all parents to contribute. A parent who can't come to school could cut out or staple things at home or contribute supplies for a project. When you're using the material prepared or contributed by those parents, highlight their contribution to let the children know that all of their families are supporting their work in important ways.

**Family Participation Ideas**

**School-Day Ideas**

- Help with messy or complicated art, science, or other projects
- Chaperone field trips
- Help make books and publish students' writing
- Share special art, language, or other expertise
- Have lunch with their child
- Do photocopying, stapling, cutting, etc.

**Evening Ideas**

- **End-of-unit celebrations.** Fairy tale plays, Readers Theater, presentations of science or social studies projects
- **Reading night or book parties.** Students share projects about books they've read
- **Math games night.** Students teach family members their favorite math games
- **Art gallery openings.** Families view a display of children's artwork

# Closing Thoughts

Thoughtful, positive communication with parents makes for a more successful school year for everyone. When we share information with parents and listen to their insights, we help them best support their child's learning. Second grade parents especially need reassurance that their child is on the right track and will appreciate some tips for responding to the changes that are common during second grade. As a teacher, you're in a unique position to help allay any concerns and guide parents to seeing the positives in their child.

# Favorite Books, Board Games, and Websites
## for Second Graders

For this appendix, I've attempted the almost impossible task of choosing a few of my current favorite books, games, and websites for second graders. I hope my choices will give you a start in planning and setting up your own classroom. Of course, I could go on and on making recommendations, as there are so many more great resources out there! But this is meant to be an introductory list, rather than an exhaustive one.

## Read-Aloud Books

### *Picture Books*

*Abuela* by Arthur Dorros, illustrated by Elisa Kleven

*All the Places to Love* by Patricia MacLachlan, illustrated by Mike Wimmer

*Chrysanthemum* by Kevin Henkes

*A Couple of Boys Have the Best Week Ever* by Marla Frazee

*Diary of a Worm* by Doreen Cronin, illustrated by Harry Bliss

*The Dinosaurs of Waterhouse Hawkins* by Barbara Kerley, illustrated by Brian Selznick

*The Disappearing Alphabet* by Richard Wilbur, illustrated by David Diaz

*Flossie and the Fox* by Patricia McKissack, illustrated by Rachel Isadora

*The Gardener* by Sarah Stewart, illustrated by David Small

*Grandfather's Journey* by Allen Say

*Halibut Jackson* by David Lucas

*I Know What You Do When I Go To School* by A. E. Cannon, illustrated by Jennifer Mazzucco

*I Love Saturdays y Domingos* by Alma Flor Ada, illustrated by Elivia Savadier

*It Could Always Be Worse* by Margot Zemach

*Loud Emily* by Alexis O'Neill, illustrated by Nancy Carpenter

*Mailing May* by Michael O. Tunnell, illustrated by Ted Rand

*Mañana, Iguana* by Ann Whitford Paul, illustrated by Ethan Long

CONTINUED

## Picture Books

*The Man Who Walked Between the Towers* by Mordicai Gerstein

*Mirette on the High Wire* by Emily Arnold McCully

*More Than Anything Else* by Marie Bradby, illustrated by Chris K. Soentpiet

*A Mother for Choco* by Keiko Kasza

*My Best Friend* by Mary Ann Rodman, illustrated by E. B. Lewis

*My Great-Aunt Arizona* by Gloria Houston, illustrated by Susan Condie Lamb

*Something Beautiful* by Sharon Dennis Wyeth, illustrated by Chris K. Soentpiet

*Superdog: The Heart of a Hero* by Caralyn Buehner, illustrated by Mark Buehner

*Table Manners* by Chris Raschka, illustrated by Vladimir Radunsky

*Tomás and the Library Lady* by Pat Mora, illustrated by Raul Colon

*Two Mrs. Gibsons* by Toyomi Igus, illustrated by Daryl Wells

## Chapter Books

*26 Fairmount Avenue* by Tomie DePaola

*Gooney Bird Greene* by Lois Lowry

*Gooseberry Park* by Cynthia Rylant

*Harriet's Hare* by Dick King-Smith

*Ruby Lu, Brave and True* by Lenore Look, illustrated by Anne Wilsdorf

*The Stories Huey Tells* by Ann Cameron

*The World According to Humphrey* by Betty G. Birney

*The Year of Miss Agnes* by Kirkpatrick Hill

# Classroom Library Books

All of the read-alouds listed above are great to stock in the classroom library. In addition, consider these favorite books:

## Fiction

(Each of these is the name of a series or the first book in a series.)

*Agapanthus Hum* by Joy Cowley

*Cam Jansen* by David A. Adler

*Dragon Slayers Academy* by Kate McMullan

*Elizabeti's Doll* by Stephanie Stuve-Bodeen

*Henry and Mudge* by Cynthia Rylant

*Hopscotch Hill School* by Valerie Tripp

*Iris and Walter* by Elissa Haden Guest

*Jackson Friends* by Michelle Edwards

*Magic Treehouse* by Mary Pope Osborne

## Fiction

*Mary Marony* by Suzy Kline

*Mercy Watson* by Kate DiCamillo

*Pinky and Rex* by James Howe

*Poppleton* by Cynthia Rylant

*Puppy Friends* by Jenny Dale

*Riverside Kids* by Johanna Hurwitz

*Secrets of Droon* by Tony Abbott

## Poetry

*all the small poems and fourteen more* by Valerie Worth, illustrated by Natalie Babbitt

*Brothers & Sisters: Family Poems* by Eloise Greenfield, illustrated by Jan Spivey Gilchrist

*The Dream Keeper and Other Poems* by Langston Hughes, illustrated by Brian Pinkney

*Falling Up* by Shel Silverstein

*Hailstones and Halibut Bones* by Mary O'Neill, illustrated by John Wallner

*Laugh-eteria* by Douglas Florian

*The New Kid on the Block* by Jack Prelutsky, illustrated by James Stevenson

*A Pocketful of Poems* by Nikki Grimes, illustrated by Javaka Steptoe

*A Poke in the I* by Paul B. Janeczko, illustrated by Chris Raschka

*Walking the Bridge of Your Nose* by Michael Rosen and Chloe Cheese

## Informational Texts and Other Nonfiction

*Cactus Hotel,* by Brenda Z. Guiberson, illustrated by Megan Lloyd

*Chameleon, Chameleon* by Joy Cowley, illustrated by Nic Bishop

*Martin's Big Words: The Life of Dr. Martin Luther King, Jr.* by Doreen Rappaport, illustrated by Bryan Collier

*Nights of the Puffling* by Bruce McMillan

*Rare Treasure: Mary Anning and Her Remarkable Discoveries* by Don Brown

*Real McCoy: The Life of an African-American Inventor* by Wendy Towle, illustrated by Wil Clay

*Simply Science* (series) by Compass Point Books

*Snowflake Bentley* by Jacqueline Briggs Martin, illustrated by Mary Azarian

*Surprising Sharks* by Nicola Davies, illustrated by James Croft

*Vote!* by Eileen Christelow

*What Do You Do With a Tail Like This?* by Robin Page, illustrated by Steve Jenkins (or other books illustrated by Steve Jenkins)

# Board Games

The Allowance Game (Lakeshore Toys)

Boggle (Parker Bros.)

Connect 4 (Hasbro)

Dino Math Tracks: A Place Value Game (Learning Resources)

Dominoes

I Spy Word Scramble Game (Briarpatch)

Mancala

Outburst (Parker Bros.)

Pictureka (Parker Bros.)

Slamwich (Gamewright)

UNO (Mattel)

# Websites

Funbrain ■ WWW.FUNBRAIN.COM  Offers a variety of interactive games across subject areas.

Learning Planet ■ WWW.LEARNINGPLANET.COM  Includes a host of interactive games (some free, more available for a yearly subscription fee).

Math Is Fun! ■ WWW.MATHISFUN.COM  Provides information about math and interactive math games.

National Geographic Kids ■ WWW.KIDS.NATIONALGEOGRAPHIC.COM  Includes a variety of interactive games and information about science and math.

VocabularySpellingCity ■ WWW.SPELLINGCITY.COM  Users can create personalized spelling and word games according to word lists.

Storyline Online ■ WWW.STORYLINEONLINE.NET  Features actors from the Screen Actors Guild reading a variety of popular picture books aloud with streaming video images of the books.

To find additional books and other resources, talk with other teachers, librarians, parents—and the children themselves.

# ACKNOWLEDGMENTS

My teaching path has crossed with those of so many gifted people. My first principal, Kathy Woods, inspired me in ways too numerous to describe, and I continue to benefit from her wisdom about children, teaching, and life. I was lucky enough to teach with many amazing second grade teachers, including Jan Maier, Molly Darr, John Holleman, Kady Folk, Kate McGowan, and Katherine Pitt. Many of the ideas and insights in this book came from them. My various assistant teachers in second grade—Bea Cope, Lara Webb, Beckie Stokes, Angie Mitchell, and Dylan Burns—provided much needed help, laughter, and wisdom. As an administrator, Babs Freeman-Loftis gave me invaluable support and continues to be a thoughtful and selfless friend and colleague. Of course, the second graders I was lucky enough to teach over the years have taught me the most important lessons about how to teach second grade.

The *Responsive Classroom®* approach changed me as a teacher and person. I'd like to thank all the professionals at Northeast Foundation for Children, especially Paula Denton, who became an amazing mentor and friend. I also want to acknowledge and thank Marlynn Clayton, who has been so kind and generous to me and whose work on one of NEFC's first books, *A Notebook for Teachers*, inspired this project. [Publisher's note: Northeast Foundation for Children is the former name of Center for Responsive Schools.]

Writing this book was fun, energizing, and blessedly uneventful, in no small part due to the help I received from many talented people. I benefited greatly from Mike Anderson's thinking and insight and from Alice Yang's and Elizabeth Nash's editing of my drafts. Their thought-provoking questions and comments made me reflect, rewrite, and laugh. I'd also like to thank Amy Treadwell for her insights when reviewing the manuscript. Thanks also to Helen Merena, whose graphic design talents made the book beautiful and accessible to readers.

I want to thank my husband Andy, who always shows genuine interest in everything I do, say, and write; listens as no one else can; and supports me in every way possible. He and our son Matthew make each day special, richer, and happier. My siblings, siblings-in-law, nieces, and nephews mean the world to me, and I want to thank them all for the many gifts they bring to my life and work. My friend Lara puts life and writing in perspective, always makes me laugh, and is just what a friend should be.

Finally, I want to thank my parents. The way they raised my six siblings and me gave me my first view of what excellent teaching looks like. Plus, they taught me to love words, work really hard, and keep my eye on things that matter.

## ABOUT THE AUTHOR

 **Margaret Berry Wilson** has used the *Reponsive Classroom*® approach to teaching since 1998. She worked for fifteen years as a classroom teacher in Nashville, Tennessee, and San Bernardino, California, before becoming a *Reponsive Classroom* consultant with Center for Responsive Schools (formerly Northeast Foundation for Children).

Margaret is the author of a number of books published by Center for Responsive Schools, including two other books in the *What Every Teacher Needs to Know* series (kindergarten and first grade), and *Doing Math in Morning Meeting: 150 Quick Activities That Connect to Your Curriculum* (with co-author Andy Dousis). She lives in Riverside, California, with her husband, Andy, and their son, Matthew.

# About the *Responsive Classroom*® Approach

All of the recommended practices in this book come from or are consistent with the *Responsive Classroom* approach to teaching—an evidence-based education approach associated with greater teacher effectiveness, higher student achievement, and improved school climate. *Responsive Classroom* practices help educators build competencies in four interrelated domains: engaging academics, positive community, effective management, and developmentally responsive teaching.

To learn more, see the following resources published by Center for Responsive Schools and available at www.responsiveclassroom.org.

*Morning Meeting:* Gather as a whole class each morning to greet each other, share news, and warm up for the day of learning ahead.

*The Morning Meeting Book*, 3rd ed., by Roxann Kriete and Carol Davis. 2014.

*80 Morning Meeting Idea Books for Grades K–2* by Susan Lattanzi Roser. 2012.

*80 Morning Meeting Idea Books for Grades 3–6* by Carol Davis. 2012.

*Doing Math in Morning Meeting: 150 Quick Activities That Connect to Your Curriculum* by Andy Dousis and Margaret Berry Wilson with an introduction by Roxann Kriete. 2010.

*Doing Science in Morning Meeting: 150 Quick Activities That Connect to Your Curriculum* by Lara Webb and Margaret Berry Wilson. 2013.

*Doing Language Arts in Morning Meeting: 150 Quick Activities That Connect to Your Curriculum* by Jodie Luongo, Joan Riordan, and Kate Umstatter. 2015.

*Doing Social Studies in Morning Meeting: 150 Quick Activities That Connect to Your Curriculum* by Leah Carson and Jane Cofie. 2017.

*Foundation-Setting During the First Weeks of School:* Take time in the critical first weeks of school to establish expectations, routines, a sense of community, and a positive classroom tone.

*The First Six Weeks of School*, 2nd ed. From *Responsive Classroom*. 2015.

**Positive Teacher Language:** Use words and tone as a tool to promote children's active learning, sense of community, and self-discipline.

*The Power of Our Words: Teacher Language That Helps Children Learn*, 2nd ed., by Paula Denton, EdD. 2014.

*Teacher Language for Engaged Learning: 4 Video Study Sessions.* 2013.

**Engaging Academics:** Learn tools for effective teaching and making lessons lively, appropriately challenging, and purposeful to help children develop higher levels of motivation, persistence, and mastery of skills and content.

*The Joyful Classroom: Practical Ways to Engage and Challenge Students K–6.* From *Responsive Classroom* with Lynn Bechtel and Kristen Vincent. 2016.

*The Language of Learning: Teaching Students Core Thinking, Speaking, and Listening Skills* by Margaret Berry Wilson. 2014.

**Special Area Educators:** Explore key *Responsive Classroom* practices adapted for a wide variety of special areas.

*Responsive Classroom for Music, Art, PE, and Other Special Areas.* From *Responsive Classroom.* 2016.

**Teaching Discipline:** Use practical strategies, such as rule creation and positive responses to misbehavior, to promote self-discipline in students and build a safe, calm, and respectful school climate.

*Teaching Self-Discipline: The Responsive Classroom Guide to Helping Students Dream, Behave, and Achieve in Elementary School.* From *Responsive Classroom* with Laurie Badge, Suzy Ghosh, Earl Hunter II, Caitie Meehan, and Cory Wade. 2018.

*Teasing, Tattling, Defiance and More: Positive Approaches to 10 Common Classroom Behaviors* by Margaret Berry Wilson. 2013.

*Responsive School Discipline: Essentials for Elementary School Leaders* by Chip Wood and Babs Freeman-Loftis. 2011.

**Classroom Management:** Set up and run a classroom in ways that enable the best possible teaching and learning.

*Interactive Modeling: A Powerful Technique for Teaching Children* by Margaret Berry Wilson. 2012.

*What Every Teacher Needs to Know*, K–5 series, by Margaret Berry Wilson and Mike Anderson. 2010–2011. (One book at each grade level.)

*Teaching Children to Care: Classroom Management for Ethical and Academic Growth K–8*, revised ed., by Ruth Sidney Charney. 2002.

**Solving Behavior Problems With Children:** Engage children in solving their behavior problems so they feel safe, challenged, and invested in changing.

*Solving Thorny Behavior Problems: How Teachers and Students Can Work Together* by Caltha Crowe. 2009.

*Sammy and His Behavior Problems: Stories and Strategies from a Teacher's Year* by Caltha Crowe. 2010.

**Preventing Bullying at School:** Use practical strategies throughout the day to create a safe, kind environment in which bullying is far less likely to take root.

*How to Bullyproof Your Classroom* by Caltha Crowe. 2012. (Includes bullying prevention lessons.)

**Movement, Games, Songs, and Chants:** Sprinkle quick, lively activities throughout the school day to keep students energized, engaged, and alert.

*99 Activities and Greetings: Great for Morning Meeting . . . and Other Meetings, Too!* by Melissa Correa-Connolly. 2004.

*Energizers! 88 Quick Movement Activities That Refresh and Refocus, K–6* by Susan Lattanzi Roser. 2009.

*Closing Circles: 50 Activities for Ending the Day in a Positive Way* by Dana Januszka and Kristen Vincent. 2012.

**Child Development:** Understand children's common physical, social-emotional, cognitive, and language characteristics at each age, and adapt teaching to respond to children's developmental needs.

*Yardsticks: Child and Adolescent Development Ages 4–14*, 4th ed., by Chip Wood. 2017.

Yardsticks Guide Series: Common Developmental Characteristics in the Classroom and at Home, Grades K–8 (from *Responsive Classroom*, 2018; based on *Yardsticks* by Chip Wood).

**Professional Development/Staff Meetings:** Learn easy-to-use structures for getting the most out of your work with colleagues.

*Energize Your Meetings! 35 Interactive Learning Structures for Educators.* From *Responsive Classroom*. 2014.

# About Child Development

Understanding children's development is crucial to teaching them well. To learn more about child development, see the following resources:

*Child and Adolescent Development for Educators* by Michael Pressley and Christine McCormick. Guilford Press. 2007. This textbook presents understandable explanations of theories and research about child development and suggests ways to apply those theories and research to classroom teaching.

*Child Development*, 8th ed., by Laura E. Berk. Pearson Education, Inc. 2009. This textbook summarizes the history and current thinking about child development in easy-to-understand prose. The author outlines the major theories and research and provides practical guidance for teachers.

*Child Development Guide* by the Center for Development of Human Services, SUNY, Buffalo State College. www.bsc-cdhs.org/fosterparent training/pdfs/childdevelguide.pdf. The center presents characteristics of children at each stage of development in an easy-to-use guide for foster parents.

"The Child in the Elementary School" by Frederick C. Howe in *Child Study Journal*, Vol. 23, Issue 4. 1993. The author presents the common characteristics of students at each grade level, identified by observing students and gathering teacher observations.

"How the Brain Learns: Growth Cycles of Brain and Mind" by Kurt W. Fischer and Samuel P. Rose in *Educational Leadership*, Vol. 56: 3, pp. 56–60. November 1998. The authors, who blend the study of child development with neuroscience, summarize their prior work in a format intended for educators. They conclude that "both behavior and the brain change in repeating patterns that seem to involve common growth cycles."

"The Scientist in the Crib: A Conversation with Andrew Meltzoff" by Marcia D'Arcangelo in *Educational Leadership*, Vol. 58: 3, pp. 8–13. November 2000. In an interview format, this article dispels myths about child development and explores ways in which research about cognitive development might inform the work of educators.

*Yardsticks: Child and Adolescent Development 4–14*, 4th ed., by Chip Wood. Center for Responsive Schools. 2017. This highly practical book for teachers and parents offers narratives and easy-to-scan charts of children's common physical, social-emotional, cognitive, and language characteristics at each age from four through fourteen and notes the classroom implications of these characteristics.

*Your Child: Emotional, Behavioral, and Cognitive Development from Birth through Preadolescence* by AACAP (American Academy of Child and Adolescent Psychiatry) and David Pruitt, MD. Harper Paperbacks. 2000. Intended for parents, this book presents information about children's development and offers tips for helping children develop appropriately.

## ABOUT THE PUBLISHER

Center for Responsive Schools, Inc., a not-for-profit educational organization, is the developer of *Responsive Classroom*®, an evidence-based education approach associated with greater teacher effectiveness, higher student achievement, and improved school climate. *Responsive Classroom* practices help educators build competencies in four interrelated domains: engaging academics, positive community, effective management, and developmentally responsive teaching. We offer the following for resources for educators:

### PROFESSIONAL DEVELOPMENT SERVICES

■ Workshops for K–8 educators (locations around the country and internationally)

■ On-site consulting services to support implementation

■ Resources for site-based study

■ Annual conferences for K–8 educators

### PUBLICATIONS AND RESOURCES

■ Books on a wide variety of *Responsive Classroom* topics

■ Free monthly newsletter

■ Extensive library of free articles on our website

### FOR DETAILS, CONTACT:

Center for Responsive Schools, Inc.
85 Avenue A, P.O. Box 718
Turners Falls, Massachusetts 01376-0718

800-360-6332 ■ www.responsiveclassroom.org
info@responsiveclassroom.org